JavaScript Handbook Core Concepts

JavaScript Foundations: Essential Concepts and Skills

By
Laurence Lars Svekis

Dedicated to
Alexis and Sebastian
Thank you for your support

For more content and to learn more, visit
https://basescripts.com/

Summary 4

Introduction 4

JavaScript Data Types and Variables 5

Multiple Choice Questions (With Answers and Explanations) 11

10 Coding Exercises with Full Solutions and Explanations 18

Conclusion 25

JavaScript Operators 26

20 Multiple-Choice Questions 32

10 Coding Exercises with Full Solutions and Explanations 38

Conclusion 44

JavaScript Control Flow 44

Multiple Choice Questions (with Answers and Explanations) 51

10 Coding Exercises with Full Solutions and Explanations 56

Conclusion 62

JavaScript Functions 63

Multiple Choice Questions (with Answers and Explanations) 69

10 Coding Exercises with Full Solutions and Explanations 74

Conclusion 80

JavaScript Scope 81

Multiple Choice Questions 86

10 Coding Exercises with Solutions and Explanations 91

Conclusion 97

JavaScript Hoisting 98

Multiple Choice Questions (With Answers and Explanations) 102

10 Coding Exercises with Solutions and Explanations 108

Conclusion 114

JavaScript Closures 114

Multiple Choice Questions (With Answers and Explanations) 118

10 Coding Exercises with Solutions and Explanations 124

Conclusion 131

JavaScript Callbacks 132

Multiple Choice Questions (With Answers and Explanations) 136

10 Coding Exercises with Solutions and Explanations 142

Conclusion 149

JavaScript Promises 150

Multiple Choice Questions (with Answers and Explanations) 154

10 Coding Exercises with Solutions and Explanations 160

Conclusion 166

Async/Await in JavaScript 167

Multiple Choice Questions 170

10 Coding Exercises with Solutions and Explanations 176

Conclusion 183

About the Author 184

Summary

The **JavaScript Handbook: Core Concepts** provides a comprehensive, hands-on approach to learning JavaScript's most essential principles. Covering topics like **data types, variables, operators, control flow, functions, closures, callbacks, promises, and asynchronous programming**, this book is an essential resource for beginners and experienced developers alike.
Each chapter is designed to break down complex concepts into easy-to-understand lessons, supported by **coding exercises, multiple-choice questions, and practical explanations**. With step-by-step guidance, readers build confidence as they progress from the basics to more advanced principles.
Whether you're preparing for a coding interview, aiming to improve your programming skills, or just starting your journey as a web developer, this book provides the essential knowledge and interactive learning experience you need to succeed.
By the end of this book, you'll have a strong grasp of **JavaScript fundamentals**, enabling you to write efficient, clean, and maintainable code. This is not just a book—it's a **complete learning experience** designed to help you achieve JavaScript mastery.

Introduction

Welcome to the **JavaScript Handbook: Core Concepts** — a comprehensive guide to mastering the building blocks of JavaScript. This book is designed to provide you with a solid foundation in JavaScript, covering essential concepts that are fundamental to every developer's journey. JavaScript is one of the most in-demand and widely used programming languages in the world, powering millions of web applications and interactive user experiences. Mastering its core concepts is a vital step toward becoming a proficient web developer. This book is designed to guide you through the essential principles of JavaScript, from **data types, variables, and operators** to more advanced topics like **scope, closures, and asynchronous programming**.

Each chapter introduces a key topic, complete with explanations, multiple-choice questions, coding exercises, and step-by-step solutions. You'll get hands-on practice to reinforce your understanding, test your knowledge, and apply what you learn in real-world development scenarios. Whether you're a beginner looking to build a strong foundation or an experienced developer aiming to fill knowledge gaps, this book will challenge you to think critically and sharpen your skills. By the end, you'll have the confidence and knowledge to write clean, efficient, and maintainable JavaScript code.

JavaScript Data Types and Variables

Introduction

In JavaScript, variables store data values. Variables themselves are containers for data, and the data they hold can be of different types. Understanding how to declare variables, what data types exist, and how they behave is fundamental to writing effective and maintainable JavaScript code.

Variable Declarations: `var`, `let`, and `const`

In modern JavaScript (ES6 and beyond), there are three ways to declare variables:
1. **var**
2. **let**
3. **const**

Each keyword affects the scope, hoisting behavior, and mutability of the variable.

`var`

- **Scope**: Function-scoped. If declared outside a function, it attaches to the global object.
- **Hoisting**: Variables declared with `var` are hoisted to the top of their scope, meaning they are accessible throughout the entire function or global context. However, they are initialized with `undefined` until their actual assignment.
- **Redeclaration**: Variables declared with `var` can be redeclared in the same scope, which can sometimes lead to bugs.

Example:

```
console.log(x); // undefined due to
hoisting, but no error
var x = 10;
console.log(x); // 10
```

`let`

- **Scope**: Block-scoped. Variables declared with `let` only exist within the nearest pair of curly braces {}.
- **Hoisting**: `let` declarations are also hoisted, but they are not initialized until their actual declaration line. Accessing them before initialization results in a `ReferenceError`.
- **Redeclaration**: You cannot redeclare a `let` variable in the same scope.

Example:

```
// console.log(y); // Would cause
ReferenceError if uncommented
let y = 20;
console.log(y); // 20

if (true) {
   let y = 30;
   console.log(y); // 30 (this is a
different 'y', block-scoped)
}
console.log(y); // 20 (original 'y')
```

const

- **Scope**: Block-scoped, similar to `let`.
- **Hoisting**: Also hoisted but not initialized until the declaration. Attempting to use a `const` variable before it is declared will cause a `ReferenceError`.
- **Immutability of Binding**: `const` variables cannot be reassigned to a new value. However, if a `const` variable holds a reference to an object or array, the contents of that object or array can still be modified.

- **Redeclaration**: Not allowed in the same scope.
Example:

```
const PI = 3.14159;
console.log(PI); // 3.14159
// PI = 3.14; // Error: Assignment to
constant variable

const arr = [1, 2, 3];
arr.push(4); // Allowed, because we're not
changing the binding, just the contents
console.log(arr); // [1, 2, 3, 4]
```

Data Types in JavaScript

JavaScript has two broad categories of data types:
1. **Primitive types**
2. **Reference types (Objects)**

Primitive Types

Primitives are data types that hold a single value. They are immutable, meaning their values cannot be changed once created. Any operation on a primitive creates a new primitive value.
The primitive types in JavaScript are:
1. **Number**: Represents both integer and floating-point numbers, e.g. `42`, `3.14`.
2. **String**: A sequence of characters enclosed in quotes, e.g. `"Hello"`, `'World'`.
3. **Boolean**: A logical entity that can be either `true` or `false`.
4. **null**: A special value that denotes "no value" or "empty".

5. **undefined**: A variable that has been declared but has not been assigned a value is `undefined`.
6. **Symbol** (ES6): A unique and immutable primitive, often used as keys for object properties.
7. **BigInt** (ES2020): Used for integers of arbitrary length, denoted by an `n` suffix, e.g. `12345678901234567890123456789 0n`.

Examples of primitives:

```
let num = 10;            // Number
let str = "JavaScript"; // String
let bool = true;         // Boolean
let nothing = null;      // null
let undef;               // undefined
(variable declared but not initialized)
let sym = Symbol("id"); // Symbol
let big = 9007199254740993n; // BigInt
```

Key characteristics of primitives:
- **Immutability**: You cannot change a primitive value directly; any operation returns a new primitive.
- **Comparison by value**: Two primitives are equal if they have the same value. For instance, `42 === 42` is `true`.

Reference Types (Objects)

Objects are collections of key-value pairs and are mutable. Arrays, functions, and most non-primitive data in JavaScript are Objects.
- **Examples of objects:**
  - Object literals: `{ name: "John", age: 30 }`
  - Arrays: `[1, 2, 3]`

○ Functions: `function greet() { console.log("Hello"); }`
○ Dates: `new Date()`
○ Regular Expressions: `/\w+/`

Key characteristics of reference types:

• **Mutability**: You can change properties or elements without creating a new object.

Comparison by reference: Two objects are equal only if they reference the same location in memory. For example:

```
let obj1 = { value: 10 };
let obj2 = { value: 10 };
console.log(obj1 === obj2); // false,
different references
let obj3 = obj1;
console.log(obj1 === obj3); // true, both
reference the same object
```
•

Choosing Between `var`, `let`, and `const`

• Use `const` by default for variables that should never be reassigned.
• Use `let` for variables that need to be reassigned later.
• Avoid `var` in modern code, as `let` and `const` provide clearer scoping and fewer pitfalls.

Additional Examples

Primitive behavior:

```
let a = 10;
let b = a; // b gets a copy of the value 10
```

```
b = 20;     // b is now 20, but a is still
10
console.log(a); // 10
console.log(b); // 20
```

Reference behavior:

```
let arr1 = [1, 2, 3];
let arr2 = arr1; // arr2 references the
same array as arr1
arr2.push(4);
console.log(arr1); // [1, 2, 3, 4]
console.log(arr2); // [1, 2, 3, 4]
```

Multiple Choice Questions (With Answers and Explanations)

1. Which of the following is NOT a primitive data type in JavaScript?
A. Number
B. String
C. Boolean
D. Object
Answer: D
Explanation: Objects are reference types, not primitives.

2. What keyword(s) can you use to declare variables in modern JavaScript?
A. var

B. let
C. const
D. All of the above
Answer: D
Explanation: You can use `var`, `let`, and `const` in JavaScript to declare variables.

3. What is the scope of a variable declared with `var` inside a function?
A. Global scope
B. Function scope
C. Block scope
D. Lexical scope
Answer: B
Explanation: Variables declared with `var` inside a function are scoped to that function.

4. Attempting to use a `let` variable before it is declared results in:
A. `undefined`
B. `ReferenceError`
C. `NaN`
D. `TypeError`
Answer: B
Explanation: `let` and `const` variables are not initialized until their declaration is evaluated, so using them beforehand results in a `ReferenceError`.

5. Which data type is used to represent values like `true` and `false`?
A. Number
B. Boolean
C. String
D. Symbol

Answer: B

Explanation: Boolean represents logical values `true` and `false`.

6. What happens if you declare a variable with `const` and then try to reassign it?

A. It changes the value successfully.

B. It throws a `ReferenceError`.

C. It throws a `TypeError`.

D. It silently fails.

Answer: C

Explanation: Reassigning a `const` variable results in a `TypeError` because `const` bindings are immutable.

7. Consider the following code:

```
var x = 5;
if (true) {
    var x = 10;
}
console.log(x);
```

What is logged to the console?

A. 5

B. 10

C. Error

D. undefined

Answer: B

Explanation: `var` is function-scoped, not block-scoped. The `var x = 10;` inside the `if` statement overwrites the outer x.

8. Consider the following code:

```
let y = 5;
if (true) {
    let y = 10;
}
console.log(y);
```

What is logged to the console?
A. 5
B. 10
C. Error
D. undefined
Answer: A
Explanation: With `let`, the y inside the `if` block is a separate variable from the outer y. Therefore, the outer y remains 5.

9. Which of the following is a valid BigInt in JavaScript?
A. `12345`
B. `12345n`
C. `BigInt(12345)`
D. Both B and C
Answer: D
Explanation: BigInt can be created by appending `n` to a number literal or by using the `BigInt()` function.

10. If `let a = { value: 10 }; let b = a;` and then `b.value = 20;`, what is `a.value`?
A. 10
B. 20
C. undefined
D. Error

Answer: B
Explanation: `a` and `b` reference the same object, so changing `b.value` also reflects in `a.value`.

11. Which keyword would you choose for a variable you know won't change values?
A. var
B. let
C. const
D. any of these
Answer: C
Explanation: `const` is used for variables that won't be reassigned.

12. `typeof null` in JavaScript returns what?
A. "null"
B. "object"
C. "undefined"
D. "number"
Answer: B
Explanation: Due to a historical quirk, `typeof null` returns "object".

13. Which of the following is block-scoped?
A. var
B. let
C. const
D. B and C
Answer: D
Explanation: Both `let` and `const` are block-scoped.

14. If you do not assign a value to a variable declared with `var`, what is its value?

A. null
B. undefined
C. NaN
D. 0
Answer: B
Explanation: A declared but uninitialized variable has the value undefined.

15. Which type is used for unique keys in objects, introduced in ES6?
A. Boolean
B. Symbol
C. Number
D. BigInt
Answer: B
Explanation: Symbols are often used as unique keys in objects.

16. What is the primary difference between primitives and objects in terms of equality?
A. Primitives are compared by value, objects by reference.
B. Objects are compared by value, primitives by reference.
C. Both are compared by reference.
D. Both are compared by value.
Answer: A
Explanation: Primitives are compared by their value; objects are compared by their reference identity.

17. Which primitive represents the intentional absence of any value?
A. undefined
B. null
C. Boolean
D. Number

Answer: B
Explanation: `null` represents a deliberate "empty" or "nothing" value.

18. Consider:

```
let p;
console.log(p);
```

What is logged?
A. null
B. undefined
C. Error
D. "" (empty string)
Answer: B
Explanation: A variable declared but not assigned is `undefined`.

19. Which variable declaration keyword does NOT allow redeclaration in the same scope?
A. var
B. let
C. const
D. B and C
Answer: D
Explanation: Neither `let` nor `const` allow redeclaration in the same scope.

20. If you want a global variable without explicitly attaching it to the window object, which keyword is least advisable to use nowadays?
A. var
B. let

C. const
D. None of the above

Answer: A

Explanation: var can cause unintended global variables and is generally discouraged in modern code. let and const are block-scoped and won't attach to the window by default.

10 Coding Exercises with Full Solutions and Explanations

1. Check Variable Scope with let and var

Problem:
Write a function that uses var and let variables, and demonstrate how they behave differently in block scopes.
Solution:

```
function variableScopeDemo() {
  var x = 10;
  if (true) {
    var x = 20; // same x variable
    let y = 30; // block-scoped variable y
    console.log("Inside block, x =", x); //
20
    console.log("Inside block, y =", y); //
30
  }
  console.log("Outside block, x =", x); //
20
```

```
  // console.log("Outside block, y =", y);
// ReferenceError: y is not defined
}

variableScopeDemo();
```

Explanation:
The `var` x inside the `if` block modifies the same x as outside. The `let` y inside the `if` block does not exist outside of that block.

2. Demonstrate `const` Immutability

Problem:
Declare a `const` variable and try to reassign it, then fix the error by using a mutable object.
Solution:

```
const PI = 3.14;
// PI = 3.1415; // This will cause a
TypeError

const person = { name: "Alice" };
person.name = "Bob"; // Allowed because we
mutate the object, not reassign 'person'
console.log(person.name); // "Bob"
```

Explanation:
`const` prevents reassignment of the variable binding. Objects referenced by a `const` can still have their properties changed.

3. Distinguish Primitives vs Objects

Problem:
Create a primitive variable and copy it. Modify the copy and show that the original is unchanged. Then do the same with an object and show that changing the copy also changes the original.
Solution:

```
// Primitive
let a = 10;
let b = a;
b = 20;
console.log(a); // 10
console.log(b); // 20

// Object
let obj1 = { value: 1 };
let obj2 = obj1;
obj2.value = 2;
console.log(obj1.value); // 2
console.log(obj2.value); // 2
```

Explanation:
Primitives are copied by value, objects by reference.

4. Using `typeof` to Identify Types

Problem:
Write code that logs the type of several variables: a number, a string, a boolean, null, undefined, and an object.

Solution:

```
let num = 42;
let str = "hello";
let bool = true;
let nothing = null;
let undef;
let arr = [1,2,3];

console.log(typeof num);     // number
console.log(typeof str);     // string
console.log(typeof bool);    // boolean
console.log(typeof nothing); // object
(quirk of JavaScript)
console.log(typeof undef);   // undefined
console.log(typeof arr);     // object
```

Explanation:
typeof helps identify data types. Note the quirk: typeof
null returns "object".

5. Block Scope with let and const

Problem:
Use a block scope to isolate a variable and ensure it's not
accessible outside.
Solution:

```
{
  let secret = "hidden message";
  const PI = 3.14159;
```

```
  console.log(secret); // "hidden message"
  console.log(PI); // 3.14159
}
// console.log(secret); // ReferenceError
// console.log(PI); // ReferenceError
```

Explanation:
let and const are block-scoped, so they can't be accessed outside their block.

6. Changing Reference vs. Changing Value in Arrays

Problem:
Create an array and assign it to another variable. Modify the second variable and show that it affects the first. Then create a new array for the second variable and show that now they are separate.
Solution:

```
let arr1 = [1, 2, 3];
let arr2 = arr1;
arr2.push(4);
console.log(arr1); // [1,2,3,4]
console.log(arr2); // [1,2,3,4]

arr2 = [9, 8, 7]; // new array assigned to
arr2
console.log(arr1); // [1,2,3,4]
console.log(arr2); // [9,8,7]
```

Explanation:
As long as arr2 references the same array, changes affect

arr1. Once arr2 is reassigned to a new array, it no longer affects arr1.

7. Use `const` with Complex Data Types

Problem:
Declare a `const` object and modify one of its properties.
Solution:

```
const config = {
   host: "localhost",
   port: 8080
};
config.port = 3000;
console.log(config.port); // 3000
```

Explanation:
The reference stored in `config` does not change, but the object's properties can be changed.

8. Hoisting with `var`

Problem:
Demonstrate hoisting by logging a `var` variable before it's declared and show what happens if you do the same with a `let` variable.
Solution:

```
// Hoisting with var
console.log(x); // undefined due to hoisting
```

```
var x = 10;
console.log(x); // 10

// console.log(y); // ReferenceError if
uncommented
let y = 20;
console.log(y); // 20
```

Explanation:
var variables are hoisted and initialized with undefined.
let variables are hoisted but not initialized, causing a
ReferenceError if accessed before declaration.

9. Using const for Configuration Constants

Problem:
Create a const variable that holds an array of allowed
extensions. Attempt to reassign the array, then just modify
its contents.
Solution:

```
const ALLOWED_EXTENSIONS = [".jpg",
".png"];
// ALLOWED_EXTENSIONS = [".gif"]; // Error:
Cannot reassign

ALLOWED_EXTENSIONS.push(".gif");
console.log(ALLOWED_EXTENSIONS); //
[".jpg", ".png", ".gif"]
```

Explanation:
You can modify the contents of an array stored in a const
variable, but you can't reassign the variable itself.

10. Understanding `typeof null`

Problem:
Write code that specifically checks if a variable is null by comparing it directly, since `typeof null` is "object".
Solution:

```
let value = null;
if (value === null) {
  console.log("The value is null");
} else {
  console.log("The value is not null");
}

console.log(typeof value); // "object"
```

Explanation:
Direct equality comparison (`=== null`) is used to check for null, because `typeof null` does not return "null".

Conclusion

Understanding variable declarations (`var`, `let`, `const`) and data types (primitives vs reference types) is crucial for writing robust and bug-free JavaScript code. Remember:
• Use `let` and `const` instead of `var` to avoid unexpected behavior.
• Primitives are immutable and compared by value.

25

- Objects (reference types) are mutable and compared by reference.
- `const` does not allow reassignment of the variable itself, but you can still mutate objects or arrays referenced by a `const` variable.

Practice the exercises, review the multiple-choice questions, and experiment with your own code to solidify these concepts.

JavaScript Operators

Introduction

Operators in JavaScript are symbols or keywords that perform operations on values (operands) and produce a result. Understanding operators and their precedence is fundamental for manipulating values and controlling the flow of your code.

Categories of JavaScript Operators

1. **Arithmetic Operators**
2. **Assignment Operators**
3. **Comparison (Relational) Operators**
4. **Logical Operators**
5. **Bitwise Operators**
6. **Ternary (Conditional) Operator**

Arithmetic Operators

These operators perform mathematical operations on numbers (and sometimes strings, for concatenation).
- **+**: Addition. Also used for string concatenation.

- -: Subtraction.
- *: Multiplication.
- /: Division.
- %: Modulus (remainder).
- **** (ES2016+): Exponentiation (e.g., 2 ** 3 === 8).
- ++: Increment by one.
- --: Decrement by one.

Examples:

```
let a = 10;
let b = 3;

console.log(a + b); // 13
console.log(a - b); // 7
console.log(a * b); // 30
console.log(a / b); // 3.3333333...
console.log(a % b); // 1 (remainder of
10/3)
console.log(2 ** 4); // 16

let x = 5;
x++;
console.log(x); // 6

let y = 5;
y--;
console.log(y); // 4
```

Note that increment (++) and decrement (--) operators can be prefix or postfix, affecting the order of evaluation.

Assignment Operators

Assignment operators assign values to variables and can also combine arithmetic operations.
- =: Basic assignment.
- +=: Addition assignment.
- -=: Subtraction assignment.
- *=: Multiplication assignment.
- /=: Division assignment.
- %=: Modulus assignment.
- **=: Exponentiation assignment (ES2016+).
- <<=, >>=, >>>=, &=, ^=, |=: Bitwise assignment operators.

Examples:

```
let c = 10;
c += 5; // c = c + 5
console.log(c); // 15

let d = 10;
d *= 2; // d = d * 2
console.log(d); // 20

let e = 10;
e **= 3; // e = e ** 3
console.log(e); // 1000
```

Comparison (Relational) Operators

These operators compare two values and return a boolean (true or false).
- ==: Equal to (loose equality, performs type coercion).

- **===**: Strict equal to (no type coercion, checks both value and type).
- **!=**: Not equal (loose inequality).
- **!==**: Strict not equal.
- **>**: Greater than.
- **>=**: Greater than or equal to.
- **<**: Less than.
- **<=**: Less than or equal to.

Examples:

```
console.log(5 == "5");  // true (type
coercion)
console.log(5 === "5"); // false (no
coercion)
console.log(3 != "3");  // false (coerced
to same value)
console.log(3 !== "3"); // true (different
types)
console.log(4 > 2);      // true
console.log(4 >= 4);     // true
console.log(2 < 3);      // true
console.log(2 <= 2);     // true
```

Logical Operators

Logical operators work with boolean values, often used in `if` statements and loops.
- **&&**: Logical AND. Returns `true` if both operands are `true`.

- ||: Logical OR. Returns `true` if at least one operand is `true`.
- !: Logical NOT. Returns `true` if the operand is `false`, and vice versa.

Examples:

```
console.log(true && false);   // false
console.log(true || false);   // true
console.log(!true);           // false
console.log(!false);          // true

// Using logical operators in conditions
let age = 25;
if (age > 18 && age < 30) {
  console.log("You're in your twenties.");
}
```

Short-Circuiting:
- && returns the first falsy value or the last value if all are truthy.
- || returns the first truthy value or the last value if none are truthy.

Example:

```
console.log("Hello" && "World"); // "World"
(both truthy, returns second)
console.log(null || "Fallback"); //
"Fallback" (null is falsy, so returns
"Fallback")
```

Bitwise Operators

Bitwise operators treat their operands as a sequence of 32 bits.

- **&**: Bitwise AND
- **|**: Bitwise OR
- **^**: Bitwise XOR
- **~**: Bitwise NOT
- **<<**: Left shift
- **>>**: Right shift
- **>>>**: Zero-fill right shift

Examples:

```
let m = 5; // binary: 0101
let n = 3; // binary: 0011

console.log(m & n); // 1 (binary: 0001)
console.log(m | n); // 7 (binary: 0111)
console.log(m ^ n); // 6 (binary: 0110)

console.log(5 << 1);  // 10 (binary: 1010)
console.log(5 >> 1);  // 2  (binary: 0010)
```

Bitwise operations are less common in daily JS coding but are useful for low-level manipulation, flags, and certain optimization scenarios.

Ternary (Conditional) Operator

The ternary operator ? : provides a concise way to write conditional expressions.
Syntax:

```
condition ? expressionIfTrue :
expressionIfFalse
```

Examples:

```
let score = 90;
let result = (score >= 60) ? "Pass" :
"Fail";
console.log(result); // "Pass"

let isMember = false;
let price = isMember ? "$5" : "$10";
console.log(price); // "$10"
```

Operator Precedence and Associativity

Operators have precedence (priority) and associativity (which direction they evaluate). For example, multiplication and division have higher precedence than addition and subtraction. Parentheses can be used to override precedence.

20 Multiple-Choice Questions

1. Which operator is used for strict equality comparison in JavaScript?
A. ==
B. ===
C. !=
D. =!

Answer: B
Explanation: === checks both the value and type without type coercion.

2. Which operator is used for string concatenation as well as addition in JavaScript?
A. +
B. *
C. &&
D. %
Answer: A
Explanation: The + operator can add numbers and also concatenate strings.

3. Which of the following operators returns the remainder after division?
A. /
B. %
C. **
D. //
Answer: B
Explanation: % returns the remainder after division.

4. What does `typeof (3 > 2)` return?
A. "boolean"
B. "number"
C. "string"
D. "undefined"
Answer: A
Explanation: 3 > 2 evaluates to true, which is a boolean.

5. Which operator can be used as a shorthand for x = x + 5?
A. x++
B. x+=5
C. x =+ 5
D. +x=5
Answer: B
Explanation: x += 5 adds 5 to x.

6. In `var result = condition ? "Yes" : "No";`, what is this operator called?
A. Logical AND
B. Nullish coalescing
C. Ternary operator
D. Bitwise operator
Answer: C
Explanation: The ? : is the ternary (conditional) operator.

7. What does `10 === "10"` evaluate to?
A. true
B. false
C. "true"
D. "false"
Answer: B
Explanation: Strict equality checks types; a number is not strictly equal to a string.

8. Which logical operator returns `true` if both operands are `true`?
A. ||
B. &&
C. !
D. ==

Answer: B
Explanation: && (logical AND) requires both operands to be truthy.

9. What is the result of 5 & 3 in binary?
A. 0b0101
B. 0b0001
C. 0b0010
D. 0b0111
Answer: B
Explanation: 5 in binary is `0101`, 3 is `0011`. `0101 & 0011 = 0001` (which is 1 in decimal).

10. What will `typeof (10 + "5")` return?
A. `"number"`
B. `"string"`
C. `"object"`
D. `"undefined"`
Answer: B
Explanation: `"5"` is a string, so `10 + "5"` is `"105"`, a string.

11. What does `!false` evaluate to?
A. false
B. true
C. null
D. undefined
Answer: B
Explanation: `!` negates the boolean; `!false` is `true`.

12. Which operator checks both value and type equality without type conversion?

A. ==
B. ===
C. =
D. !=
Answer: B
Explanation: === is strict equality checking.

13. Which operator would you use to check if x is less than or equal to y?
A. x < y
B. x <= y
C. x =< y
D. x <> y
Answer: B
Explanation: <= checks if x is less than or equal to y.

14. What is the result of 2 ** 3 in JavaScript?
A. 6
B. 8
C. 2
D. 3
Answer: B
Explanation: 2 ** 3 = 2 to the power of 3 = 8.

15. Which logical operator returns the first truthy operand or the last operand if none are truthy?
A. &&
B. ||
C. !
D. ? :
Answer: B
Explanation: The OR (||) operator returns the first truthy value or the last if none are truthy.

16. Consider `let x = 5; let y = x++;` what is the value of `y` after this operation?

A. 4

B. 5

C. 6

D. undefined

Answer: B

Explanation: `x++` returns the original value (5) before incrementing. So `y = 5`.

17. Which operator would you use to invert all the bits of a number?

A. &

B. |

C. ~

D. ^

Answer: C

Explanation: ~ is the bitwise NOT operator, inverting all bits.

18. Which operator can be used to perform exponentiation in older JavaScript engines before ** was introduced?

A. `Math.pow(x, y)`

B. `x ^ y`

C. `x * y * y`

D. `x ** y`

Answer: A

Explanation: Before **, `Math.pow()` was used for exponentiation.

19. What does `10 % 3` evaluate to?
A. 1
B. 3
C. 0
D. undefined
Answer: A
Explanation: The remainder of dividing 10 by 3 is 1.

20. In `let output = isValid ? "Valid" : "Invalid"`; what happens if `isValid` is `true`?
A. `output` will be `"Invalid"`
B. `output` will be `true`
C. `output` will be `"Valid"`
D. `output` will remain undefined
Answer: C
Explanation: The ternary operator will choose `"Valid"` if `isValid` is `true`.

10 Coding Exercises with Full Solutions and Explanations

1. Using Arithmetic and Assignment Operators

Problem:
Initialize a variable with a number. Add 10 to it, then multiply it by 2, using compound assignment operators. Print the result.
Solution:

```
let num = 5;
num += 10; // num = 15
```

```
num *= 2;   // num = 30
console.log(num); // 30
```

Explanation:
We used += and *= to modify num in place.

2. Comparing Values with Strict Equality

Problem:
Check if a string number is strictly equal to a number using
===. Print true or false.
Solution:

```
let strNum = "10";
let realNum = 10;
console.log(strNum === realNum); // false
```

Explanation:
"10" is a string, 10 is a number, so strict equality is
false.

3. Using the Ternary Operator

Problem:
Set a variable score. Use a ternary operator to assign
"Pass" to a variable status if score >= 50 else
"Fail".
Solution:

```
let score = 75;
```

```
let status = (score >= 50) ? "Pass" :
"Fail";
console.log(status); // "Pass"
```

Explanation:
The ternary checks the condition and selects one of two strings.

4. Logical Operators in Conditions

Problem:
Check if a variable `age` is between 18 and 30 using `&&`. Print `"Young Adult"` if true, otherwise print `"Not in range"`.
Solution:

```
let age = 25;
if (age >= 18 && age <= 30) {
  console.log("Young Adult");
} else {
  console.log("Not in range");
}
```

Explanation:
Both conditions must be true to print `"Young Adult"`.

5. Using || for Fallback Values

Problem:
Create a variable `username` that may be `null`. Use `||` to print a fallback username `"Guest"` if `username` is falsy.
Solution:

```
let username = null;
let displayName = username || "Guest";
console.log(displayName); // "Guest"
```

Explanation:
|| returns the second operand if the first is falsy.

6. Bitwise Operations

Problem:
Take two numbers and perform a bitwise AND & to print
the result.
Solution:

```
let p = 10;   // binary 1010
let q = 6;    // binary 0110
let r = p & q;
console.log(r); // 2 (binary 0010)
```

Explanation:
Bitwise AND takes the bits of both numbers and returns 1
only if both bits are 1.

7. Increment and Decrement Operators

Problem:
Initialize count to 0. Print it, then use count++, print
again, then use ++count, and print again.
Solution:

```
let count = 0;
console.log(count);     // 0
console.log(count++); // 0 (prints old
value, then increments)
console.log(count);     // 1
console.log(++count); // 2 (increments
first, then prints)
```

Explanation:
Postfix increments after printing, prefix increments before printing.

8. Checking Odd or Even Using the Modulus Operator

Problem:
Set a number, use % to determine if it's odd or even. Print "Even" or "Odd".
Solution:

```
let number = 7;
if (number % 2 === 0) {
   console.log("Even");
} else {
   console.log("Odd");
}
```

Explanation:
If the remainder when divided by 2 is 0, it's even; otherwise, it's odd.

9. Using Comparison in a Condition

Problem:
Compare two variables a and b. If a > b, print "a is greater". Otherwise print "b is greater or equal".
Solution:

```
let a = 10;
let b = 5;
if (a > b) {
  console.log("a is greater");
} else {
  console.log("b is greater or equal");
}
```

Explanation:
We use the greater-than operator to compare a and b.

10. Combining Multiple Operators

Problem:
Take a variable x = 2. Compute (x + 3) * 4, then check if the result is strictly equal to 20. Use a ternary operator to print "Correct" or "Incorrect".
Solution:

```
let x = 2;
let calc = (x + 3) * 4; // (2+3)*4 = 5*4 = 20
let message = (calc === 20) ? "Correct" : "Incorrect";
console.log(message); // "Correct"
```

Explanation:
We used arithmetic operations, then a strict comparison, and finally a ternary operator.

Conclusion

Operators are the building blocks of any programming language. In JavaScript:
- **Arithmetic operators** handle mathematical calculations.
- **Assignment operators** simplify the process of updating variable values.
- **Comparison operators** compare values and return booleans.
- **Logical operators** combine or invert boolean conditions.
- **Bitwise operators** work at the binary level.
- **The ternary operator** provides a concise way to return one of two values based on a condition.

By mastering these operators and understanding their precedence, you will write more efficient, clear, and bug-free JavaScript code.

JavaScript Control Flow

Introduction

Control flow statements dictate how code executes in a JavaScript program. By using conditional statements and loops, you can make the program respond to different inputs and conditions, and perform repetitive tasks without manually writing the same code multiple times.

Conditional Statements: `if`, `else if`, and `else`

`if` Statement

The `if` statement executes a block of code only if a specified condition is `true`.

Syntax:

```
if (condition) {
  // Code runs if condition is true
}
```

Example:

```
let score = 75;
if (score > 60) {
  console.log("You passed the test!");
}
```

`if-else` Statement

The `if-else` structure allows you to execute one block if the condition is `true` and another block if it's `false`.

Syntax:

```
if (condition) {
  // code if true
} else {
  // code if false
}
```

Example:

```
let age = 16;
if (age >= 18) {
  console.log("You can vote.");
} else {
  console.log("You are too young to
vote.");
}
```

if-else if-else Ladder
For multiple conditions, you can chain if and else if
statements. The first condition that is true gets executed,
and the rest are skipped.
Syntax:

```
if (condition1) {
  // code if condition1 is true
} else if (condition2) {
  // code if condition2 is true
} else {
  // code if none of the above conditions
are true
}
```

Example:

```
let grade = 85;
if (grade >= 90) {
  console.log("A");
} else if (grade >= 80) {
  console.log("B");
} else if (grade >= 70) {
  console.log("C");
```

```
} else {
  console.log("Fail");
}
```

switch-case Statement

The `switch` statement is a more readable alternative to multiple `if-else if` statements when checking one variable against many possible values.

Syntax:

```
switch (expression) {
  case value1:
    // code if expression === value1
    break;
  case value2:
    // code if expression === value2
    break;
  default:
    // code if no cases match
}
```

Example:

```
let day = 3;
switch (day) {
  case 1:
    console.log("Monday");
    break;
  case 2:
```

```
    console.log("Tuesday");
    break;
  case 3:
    console.log("Wednesday");
    break;
  default:
    console.log("Unknown day");
    break;
}
```

If you omit break, execution continues to the next case —
a behavior called "fall-through".

Loops

Loops repeat a block of code as long as a condition remains
true.

for Loop

Use a for loop when you know exactly how many
iterations you need.
Syntax:

```
for (initialization; condition; increment)
{
  // code to run each iteration
}
```

Example:

```
for (let i = 0; i < 5; i++) {
  console.log("Iteration:", i);
```

```
}
```

Flow of a for loop:
1. Initialization: run once before the loop starts.
2. Condition: checked before each iteration; if `false`, loop stops.
3. Increment: executed after each iteration.
4. Body: code runs if condition is `true`.

while Loop

Use a `while` loop when you want to loop until a certain condition changes, and you might not know the exact number of iterations upfront.
Syntax:

```
while (condition) {
  // code runs as long as condition is true
}
```

Example:

```
let count = 0;
while (count < 3) {
  console.log("Count is:", count);
  count++;
}
```

do-while Loop

A `do-while` loop runs at least once, even if the condition is initially `false`.

Syntax:

```
do {
  // code runs at least once
} while (condition);
```

Example:

```
let num = 5;
do {
  console.log("Number:", num);
  num++;
} while (num < 3);
```

In this case, the code inside do runs once before checking the condition num < 3.

Breaking and Continuing in Loops

break: Terminates the loop immediately.
continue: Skips the current iteration and continues with the next one.
Example with break:

```
for (let i = 0; i < 10; i++) {
  if (i === 5) {
    break; // stops the loop
  }
  console.log(i);
}
```

Example with continue:

```
for (let i = 0; i < 5; i++) {
  if (i === 2) {
    continue; // skip printing 2
  }
  console.log(i);
}
```

Multiple Choice Questions (with Answers and Explanations)

1. Which statement executes code only if a condition is true?
A. if
B. else
C. switch
D. do-while
Answer: A
Explanation: if executes code only if the given condition is true.

2. Which keyword is used to stop a switch case from falling through?
A. stop
B. break
C. end
D. return
Answer: B
Explanation: break stops execution of the current case block in a switch statement.

3. Which loop guarantees at least one execution of its body, regardless of the condition?

A. for

B. while

C. do-while

D. foreach

Answer: C

Explanation: `do-while` executes the body before checking the condition.

4. What is the purpose of the `continue` statement in a loop?

A. End the loop completely

B. Skip the current iteration and continue with the next

C. Repeat the current iteration

D. None of the above

Answer: B

Explanation: `continue` skips the rest of the current iteration and moves to the next iteration.

5. Which of the following is the correct syntax for a `for` loop?

A. `for i < 10 { ... }`

B. `for (i = 0; i < 10; i++) { ... }`

C. `for (i; i < 10; i++) { ... }`

D. `loop (i = 0; i < 10; i++) { ... }`

Answer: B

Explanation: The classic `for` loop syntax is `for (initialization; condition; increment) { ... }`.

6. If `if (x > 5) { console.log("x is big"); } else { console.log("x is small"); }` and `x = 10`, what prints?

A. x is big

B. x is small

C. nothing

D. Error
Answer: A
Explanation: Since x = 10 is greater than 5, it prints "x is big".
7. In a `switch` statement, what is the purpose of `default`?
A. It sets a default value for the variable.
B. It runs if no other case matches.
C. It must always be declared.
D. It is only for number cases.
Answer: B
Explanation: `default` runs if no other case matches the switch expression.
8. Which loop is best used when the number of iterations is known beforehand?
A. for
B. while
C. do-while
D. if
Answer: A
Explanation: `for` loops are typically used when the number of iterations is known.
9. How do you force an immediate exit from a loop?
A. continue
B. break
C. exit
D. return
Answer: B
Explanation: `break` stops the loop immediately.
10. What does the condition in a `while` loop control?
A. Number of times initialization runs
B. Whether the loop runs at all
C. The increment

D. Nothing

Answer: B

Explanation: The condition determines if the loop body executes or stops.

11. If you don't include a `break` in a `case` of a `switch`, what happens?

A. It throws an error.

B. Execution continues to the next case.

C. The switch ends immediately.

D. The default case is called.

Answer: B

Explanation: Without `break`, execution "falls through" to the next case.

12. Which statement is used to skip to the next iteration of a loop without finishing the current one?

A. break

B. continue

C. skip

D. pass

Answer: B

Explanation: `continue` skips the current iteration.

13. In an `if-else if-else` ladder, what happens when one condition is true?

A. Other conditions are still checked.

B. Only that condition's block executes and then the ladder ends.

C. The program continues to the else.

D. None of the above.

Answer: B

Explanation: Once a true condition is found, that block executes and no other conditions are checked.

14. Which loop checks its condition before executing the body?

A. do-while

B. while

C. switch

D. if

Answer: B

Explanation: `while` checks the condition before running the loop body.

15. The `if` statement evaluates a condition and executes the code if the condition is:

A. truthy

B. falsy

C. null

D. undefined

Answer: A

Explanation: If the condition is truthy, the `if` block executes.

16. How many times will a `for (let i = 0; i < 3; i++) { console.log(i); }` loop run?

A. 1

B. 2

C. 3

D. 4

Answer: C

Explanation: It runs for i=0, i=1, and i=2.

17. Which of the following is a valid `switch` statement snippet?

A. `switch x { case 5: ... }`

B. `switch (x) { case 5: ... }`

C. `switch x: { case 5: ... }`

D. `switch (x) case 5: { ... }`

Answer: B

Explanation: `switch (expression) { case value: ... }` is the correct syntax.

18.   Can `if` statements be nested within one another?

A. Yes, you can have if inside if

B. No, nested if is not allowed

C. Only if you have else after each if

D. Only in strict mode

Answer: A

Explanation: You can nest `if` statements as needed.

19.   Which loop is best suited for iterating until a certain condition becomes false, and you don't know the exact number of iterations?

A. for

B. while

C. do-while

D. switch

Answer: B

Explanation: `while` loops are good for unknown iteration counts.

20.   `break` can be used inside a:

A. if statement

B. function

C. switch or loop

D. variable assignment

Answer: C

Explanation: `break` works within `switch` or loops.

10 Coding Exercises with Full Solutions and Explanations

1. Simple `if` Condition

Problem:
Write code that checks if a variable x is positive. If yes,
print "Positive". Otherwise, print "Not positive".
Solution:

```
let x = 10;
if (x > 0) {
  console.log("Positive");
} else {
  console.log("Not positive");
}
```

Explanation:
We use if to check if x is greater than 0. If not, the else
block runs.

2. if-else if-else Ladder

Problem:
Given a score variable, print "A" if score >= 90, "B" if
score >= 80, "C" if score >= 70, otherwise print "F".
Solution:

```
let score = 85;
if (score >= 90) {
  console.log("A");
} else if (score >= 80) {
  console.log("B");
} else if (score >= 70) {
  console.log("C");
} else {
```

```
  console.log("F");
}
```

Explanation:
We chain multiple `else if` conditions for different score ranges.

3. Using `switch-case`

Problem:
Use a `switch` statement on variable `fruit = "apple"`. If `apple`, print "Apples are red". If `banana`, print "Bananas are yellow". For anything else, print "Unknown fruit".
Solution:

```
let fruit = "apple";
switch (fruit) {
  case "apple":
    console.log("Apples are red");
    break;
  case "banana":
    console.log("Bananas are yellow");
    break;
  default:
    console.log("Unknown fruit");
    break;
}
```

Explanation:
`switch` checks `fruit` against each `case`.

4. A Basic `for` Loop

Problem:
Print numbers from 1 to 5 using a `for` loop.
Solution:

```
for (let i = 1; i <= 5; i++) {
   console.log(i);
}
```

Explanation:
i starts at 1, runs until i <= 5, incrementing by 1 each time.

5. Summation with a `for` Loop

Problem:
Use a `for` loop to sum the numbers from 1 to 10 and print the result.
Solution:

```
let sum = 0;
for (let i = 1; i <= 10; i++) {
   sum += i;
}
console.log(sum); // 55
```

Explanation:
We keep adding i to sum each iteration.

6. Using `while` Loop

Problem:
Use a while loop to print "Hello" 3 times.
Solution:

```
let count = 0;
while (count < 3) {
  console.log("Hello");
  count++;
}
```

Explanation:
The condition checks count < 3. Each loop increments count.

7. Using do-while Loop

Problem:
Use a do-while loop to print "Run once" even if the condition is false.
Solution:

```
let shouldRun = false;
do {
  console.log("Run once");
} while (shouldRun);
```

Explanation:
The code runs once before checking the condition.

8. break in a Loop

Problem:
Write a loop from i = 0 to 9, but stop when i is 5 using
break.
Solution:

```
for (let i = 0; i < 10; i++) {
  if (i === 5) {
    break;
  }
  console.log(i);
}
```

Explanation:
When i equals 5, break ends the loop prematurely.

9. continue in a Loop

Problem:
Print numbers from 0 to 4 but skip i = 2 using
continue.
Solution:

```
for (let i = 0; i < 5; i++) {
  if (i === 2) {
    continue;
  }
  console.log(i);
}
// Prints 0,1,3,4
```

Explanation:
When i is 2, continue skips printing and moves to the next iteration.

10. Nested if Statements

Problem:
Check if a number num is positive. If it is, then further check if it's greater than 100. Print "Big Positive" if more than 100, otherwise "Small Positive". If not positive, print "Non-positive".
Solution:

```
let num = 150;
if (num > 0) {
  // Nested if
  if (num > 100) {
    console.log("Big Positive");
  } else {
    console.log("Small Positive");
  }
} else {
  console.log("Non-positive");
}
```

Explanation:
We nest another if inside the first if to refine the condition.

Conclusion

JavaScript control flow statements (`if-else`, `switch`, `for`, `while`, `do-while`) give you the power to dictate how your code runs and how it reacts to different inputs and conditions. Mastering these tools allows you to write dynamic and efficient programs that can handle any scenario.

- Use `if-else` and `switch` to handle conditions and branches.
- Use loops (`for`, `while`, `do-while`) to handle repetitive tasks.
- Employ `break` and `continue` to control loop execution flow.

By practicing the exercises and reviewing the multiple-choice questions, you should now have a solid understanding of control flow in JavaScript.

JavaScript Functions

Introduction

Functions are reusable blocks of code designed to perform a particular task. They allow you to modularize your code, improve readability, and reduce repetition. In JavaScript, there are several ways to define functions, each with its own nuances and use cases.

Function Declarations

A function declaration defines a named function using the `function` keyword followed by a name, a list of parameters in parentheses, and a block of code.

Syntax:

```
function functionName(param1, param2, ...)
{
  // function body
  // return statement (optional)
}
```

Example:

```
function greet(name) {
   console.log("Hello, " + name + "!");
}

greet("Alice"); // Output: Hello, Alice!
```

Key points about function declarations:
• They are hoisted to the top of their scope, meaning you can call them before they are defined in the code.
• The function name is mandatory and should be a valid identifier.

Function Expressions

A function expression is when you assign an anonymous (or named) function to a variable. Unlike function declarations, function expressions are not hoisted, so you can't call them before they are defined.
Syntax:

```
const myFunction = function(param) {
  // function body
};
```

Example:

```
const add = function(a, b) {
  return a + b;
};
```

```
console.log(add(2, 3)); // 5
```

Key points about function expressions:
- They can be anonymous or named.
- They are not hoisted like function declarations, so you must define them before using.
- They can be passed as arguments to other functions or returned from functions (higher-order functions).

Arrow Functions

Arrow functions, introduced in ES6, provide a concise syntax for writing functions. They are always anonymous and have a lexical `this` binding, meaning they do not create their own `this` context.

Syntax:

```
const functionName = (param1, param2) => {
  // function body
  return result;
};
```

If the function body has a single expression, and you want to return its value, you can omit the `return` keyword and the curly braces:

```
const multiply = (a, b) => a * b;
```

Examples:

```
// Single-line arrow function
const square = x => x * x;
console.log(square(4)); // 16

// Multi-line arrow function
const greet = (name) => {
  const message = "Hello, " + name;
  return message;
};
console.log(greet("Bob")); // Hello, Bob
```

Key points about arrow functions:
• They do not bind their own `this`; `this` refers to the enclosing lexical scope.
• They are shorter and often cleaner than traditional function expressions.
• They cannot be used as constructors and do not have a `prototype` property.

Immediately Invoked Function Expression (IIFE)

An IIFE is a function that runs immediately after it's defined. It's often used to create a private scope and avoid polluting the global namespace.
Syntax:

```
(function() {
  // code here runs immediately
```

```
})();
```

or with arrow functions:

```
(() => {
  console.log("IIFE runs immediately!");
})();
```

Example:

```
(function() {
  const secret = "I am hidden from the
global scope.";
  console.log("IIFE executed!");
})();

// console.log(secret); // ReferenceError:
secret is not defined
```

Key points about IIFEs:
- They create a new scope.
- Variables defined inside are not accessible outside.
- They execute as soon as the interpreter encounters them.

Parameters and Arguments

Parameters are variables listed as a part of the function definition, while **arguments** are the values passed to the function when it is invoked.
Default Parameters (ES6+): You can assign default values to parameters:

```javascript
function greet(name = "Guest") {
  console.log("Hello, " + name);
}
greet(); // Hello, Guest
```

Rest Parameters (ES6+): Use the rest parameter syntax (`...args`) to accept an indefinite number of arguments:

```javascript
function sum(...numbers) {
  return numbers.reduce((total, num) =>
total + num, 0);
}

console.log(sum(1,2,3,4)); // 10
```

Return Values

Functions can return a value using the `return` keyword. If no `return` is specified, the function returns `undefined`.
Example:

```javascript
function subtract(a, b) {
  return a - b;
}
let result = subtract(10, 3);
console.log(result); // 7
```

Higher-Order Functions and Callbacks

A **higher-order function** is a function that takes another function as an argument, or returns a function as a result.
Example:

```
function map(arr, fn) {
  const result = [];
  for (let val of arr) {
    result.push(fn(val));
  }
  return result;
}

const doubled = map([1,2,3], x => x * 2);
console.log(doubled); // [2,4,6]
```

Multiple Choice Questions (with Answers and Explanations)

1. Which of the following defines a named function in JavaScript? A. `function myFunc() { ... }`
B. `const myFunc = function() { ... }`
C. `const myFunc = () => { ... }`
D. All of the above
Answer: A
Explanation: Only `function myFunc() { ... }` is a function declaration with a name. The others are function expressions or arrow functions assigned to variables.
2. Which functions are hoisted in JavaScript? A. Function declarations

69

B. Function expressions

C. Arrow functions

D. IIFEs

Answer: A

Explanation: Function declarations are hoisted, allowing them to be called before their definition.

3. Which syntax correctly defines an arrow function that returns the sum of two numbers a and b? A. `const sum = (a, b) => { return a + b; }`

B. `const sum = (a, b) => a + b;`

C. Both A and B

D. None of the above

Answer: C

Explanation: Both forms are correct. The second form is a concise arrow function.

4. What does an IIFE do? A. Declares a function for later use

B. Immediately invokes itself upon definition

C. Binds a `this` context

D. Returns a promise

Answer: B

Explanation: IIFEs run right after they are defined.

5. Which of the following function types does not create its own `this`? A. Function declaration

B. Function expression

C. Arrow function

D. IIFE

Answer: C

Explanation: Arrow functions do not have their own `this`; they inherit it from the enclosing lexical scope.

6. If a function does not explicitly return a value, what is the default return value? A. `null`

B. `undefined`

C. `0`

D. `false`
Answer: B
Explanation: Without a `return` statement, functions return `undefined`.
7. How do you create a function that can be invoked immediately without being explicitly called later? A. Wrap it in parentheses followed by ()
B. Use `function immediate()` and call `immediate()`
C. Return it from another function
D. Use `this` keyword
Answer: A
Explanation: `(() => { ... })()` is an example of an IIFE.
8. Consider `const greet = function() { console.log("Hi"); };`. What is `greet`? A. Function declaration
B. Function expression
C. Arrow function
D. IIFE
Answer: B
Explanation: A function is assigned to a variable, making it a function expression.
9. How do default parameters work? A. They must be the first parameter
B. They provide a default value if no argument is supplied
C. They throw an error if no argument is given
D. They cannot be used with arrow functions
Answer: B
Explanation: Default parameters allow setting a default value if no argument is passed.
10. Can you call a function expression before it's defined?
A. Yes, because of hoisting
B. No, function expressions are not hoisted like

declarations

C. Only if using `var`

D. Only if using arrow functions

Answer: B

Explanation: Function expressions are not hoisted, so they must be defined before being called.

11. What does the `return` statement do inside a function? A. Stops the function's execution and returns a value

B. Prints the value on the console

C. Continues to the next line of code

D. None of the above

Answer: A

Explanation: `return` ends the function and sends a value back to the caller.

12. Which of these is a valid arrow function with no parameters? A. `const fn = => {}`

B. `const fn = () => {}`

C. `const fn = -> {}`

D. `const fn = [] => {}`

Answer: B

Explanation: Arrow functions with no parameters use empty parentheses: `() => {}`.

13. Which keyword is used to define a function declaration? A. `function`

B. `fn`

C. `arrow`

D. `def`

Answer: A

Explanation: `function` is the keyword used for declarations.

14. What is a higher-order function? A. A function that returns a string

B. A function that takes or returns another function

C. A function that runs only once
D. A function that is always anonymous
Answer: B
Explanation: Higher-order functions operate on other functions, either taking them as arguments or returning them.
15. Which of the following is NOT true about IIFEs? A. They run as soon as they are defined
B. They prevent variable pollution of the global scope
C. They can be named functions
D. They are often wrapped in parentheses
Answer: C
Explanation: IIFEs are typically anonymous and run immediately; naming them is possible but not common.
16. What happens if you use `this` inside an arrow function? A. It refers to the arrow function's own context
B. It throws an error
C. It refers to the surrounding lexical scope's `this`
D. It always refers to the global object
Answer: C
Explanation: Arrow functions do not bind their own `this`; they use the enclosing scope's `this`.
17. Can a function return another function? A. Yes, functions are first-class citizens in JavaScript
B. No, that's not allowed
C. Only arrow functions can do that
D. Only if you use `return functionName;`
Answer: A
Explanation: Functions can return other functions, making them higher-order functions.
18. When should you use a function declaration over a function expression? A. When you need hoisting or a named function

B. When you need a lexical `this`

C. When you want an IIFE

D. When you want an anonymous function

Answer: A

Explanation: Function declarations are hoisted and named, which can be beneficial in certain code structures.

What is the output of:

```
(function() {
  let message = "Hello";
  console.log(message);
})();
```

19.   A. `Hello`

B. `undefined`

C. Error

D. Nothing

Answer: A

Explanation: The IIFE logs "Hello" immediately.

20.   Consider `const double = x => x * 2;`. What is `double(5)`? A. 10

B. 2

C. `x * 2`

D. Error

Answer: A

Explanation: `double(5)` returns 5 * 2 = 10.

10 Coding Exercises with Full Solutions and Explanations

1. Basic Function Declaration

Problem:
Write a function declaration `greet` that takes a `name` parameter and prints `"Hello, name"`.
Solution:

```
function greet(name) {
  console.log("Hello, " + name);
}

greet("Alice"); // "Hello, Alice"
```

Explanation:
A simple function that uses a parameter and logs a greeting.

2. Function Expression

Problem:
Create a function expression called `add` that returns the sum of two numbers.
Solution:

```
const add = function(a, b) {
  return a + b;
};

console.log(add(3,4)); // 7
```

Explanation:
The function expression is stored in a variable `add`.

3. Arrow Function

Problem:
Convert this function declaration into an arrow function:

```
function square(x) {
    return x * x;
}
```

Solution:

```
const square = x => x * x;
console.log(square(5)); // 25
```

Explanation:
Arrow functions with one parameter don't need parentheses. Single-line return can omit `return`.

4. Default Parameters

Problem:
Write a function `multiply` that has default parameters `a` = 1 and `b` = 1. If no arguments are passed, return 1.
Solution:

```
function multiply(a = 1, b = 1) {
    return a * b;
}
```

```
console.log(multiply());     // 1*1 = 1
console.log(multiply(5));    // 5*1 = 5
console.log(multiply(3,4));  // 12
```

Explanation:
Default parameters ensure a default value if none is provided.

5. IIFE Example

Problem:
Create an IIFE that prints `"IIFE executed!"` immediately.
Solution:

```
(function() {
  console.log("IIFE executed!");
})();
```

Explanation:
The function runs right away without needing an explicit call.

6. Rest Parameters

Problem:
Write a function `sumAll` that uses rest parameters to sum any number of arguments.
Solution:

```
function sumAll(...nums) {
  return nums.reduce((total, num) => total
+ num, 0);
}
```

```
console.log(sumAll(1,2,3,4)); // 10
```

Explanation:
...nums gathers all arguments into an array, which we then reduce.

7. Returning a Function

Problem:
Write a function createMultiplier that takes a number factor and returns a new function that multiplies its argument by factor.
Solution:

```
function createMultiplier(factor) {
   return function(x) {
      return x * factor;
   };
}

const double = createMultiplier(2);
console.log(double(5)); // 10
```

Explanation:
A higher-order function that returns another function.

8. Named Function Expression

Problem:
Create a named function expression const factorial = function fact(n) {...} that returns the factorial of n.

Solution:

```
const factorial = function fact(n) {
  if (n <= 1) return 1;
  return n * fact(n - 1);
};

console.log(factorial(5)); // 120
```

Explanation:
A named function expression can call itself recursively.

9. Arrow Function with Multiple Lines

Problem:
Write an arrow function greetUser that takes name and
returns a string "Welcome, name!". Use a multi-line
arrow function body.
Solution:

```
const greetUser = (name) => {
  const message = "Welcome, " + name + "!";
  return message;
};

console.log(greetUser("Dave")); //
"Welcome, Dave!"
```

Explanation:
Arrow function with curly braces requires an explicit
return.

10. Higher-Order Function Using Arrow Functions

Problem:
Write a function `filterArray(arr, fn)` that returns a new array of elements for which `fn` returns true. Use arrow functions.
Solution:

```
function filterArray(arr, fn) {
  const result = [];
  for (let val of arr) {
    if (fn(val)) {
      result.push(val);
    }
  }
  return result;
}

const isEven = x => x % 2 === 0;
console.log(filterArray([1,2,3,4,5,6],
isEven)); // [2,4,6]
```

Explanation:
`filterArray` takes a function `fn` and applies it to each element, returning only those that pass the test.

Conclusion

Functions are at the heart of JavaScript programming. Understanding how to define them using different syntaxes—function declarations, expressions, arrow functions, and IIFEs—lets you write more modular and maintainable code. Mastering concepts like default parameters, rest parameters, higher-order functions, and lexical scoping of arrow functions will enhance your coding skills significantly.

By reviewing the examples, practicing the exercises, and understanding the nuances through the multiple-choice questions, you've now gained a comprehensive grasp of JavaScript functions.

JavaScript Scope

Introduction

Scope in JavaScript refers to the accessibility of variables and functions at various parts of your code. Understanding scope is fundamental because it determines where variables and functions can be accessed and modified. JavaScript has evolved over time, and the introduction of `let` and `const` in ES6 added block scope to the language, alongside the traditional function scope that existed with `var`. There are several types of scope in JavaScript:

1. **Global Scope**
2. **Function (Local) Scope**
3. **Block Scope**
4. **Lexical Scope** (related to closures and nested functions)

Global Scope

Variables declared outside any function or block have global scope. They are accessible anywhere in your code, even in different script files (assuming they're loaded in the same global context, like a browser window).
Example:

```
var globalVar = "I'm global!";

function printGlobal() {
  console.log(globalVar); // Accessible
inside the function
}

printGlobal(); // "I'm global!"
console.log(globalVar);   // "I'm global!"
(accessible outside too)
```

Key points:
• Global variables are properties of the global object (`window` in browsers).
• Overuse of global variables can lead to naming collisions and harder-to-maintain code.

Function Scope

Before ES6, JavaScript only had function scope. Variables declared with `var` inside a function are scoped to that function and cannot be accessed outside it.
Example:

```
function myFunction() {
  var functionVar = "I'm local to this
function";
```

```
  console.log(functionVar); // Works here
}
```

```
// console.log(functionVar); //
ReferenceError: functionVar is not defined
```

Key points:
• Variables declared with `var` inside a function are local to that function.
• Functions can access variables defined in their outer scopes due to lexical scoping.

Block Scope

With the introduction of `let` and `const`, JavaScript gained true block-level scope. A **block** is defined by `{ ... }`.
Example:

```
if (true) {
  let blockVar = "I'm only accessible
inside this block";
  console.log(blockVar); // "I'm only
accessible inside this block"
}
// console.log(blockVar); // ReferenceError
```

Key points:
• `let` and `const` are block-scoped. They exist only within the nearest set of `{ }`.
• `var` does not respect block scope, only function scope.

Lexical Scope

Lexical scope means that the scope of variables is determined by their location in the source code. Inner functions have access to variables declared in their outer functions or the global scope. This concept underpins **closures**.
Example:

```
function outer() {
  let outerVar = "Outer";

  function inner() {
    console.log(outerVar); // Inner has
access to outerVar due to lexical scope
  }

  inner(); // "Outer"
}
outer();
```

Key point:
• Lexical scope is about where variables are declared, not where functions are called.

Variable Shadowing

If a variable is declared in an inner scope with the same name as a variable in an outer scope, the inner variable **shadows** the outer one.
Example:

```
let x = 10;
```

```
function test() {
  let x = 20;
  console.log(x); // 20 (the outer x = 10
is shadowed inside the function)
}
test();
console.log(x); // 10
```

Hoisting and Scope

var variables are hoisted to the top of their function scope but initialized with **undefined** until assigned. **let** and **const** are hoisted too, but not initialized, resulting in the "Temporal Dead Zone" if accessed before declaration.
Example:

```
console.log(aVar); // undefined (var is
hoisted)
var aVar = 5;

// console.log(bLet); // ReferenceError:
Cannot access before initialization
let bLet = 10;
```

Summary

- **Global Scope**: Variables accessible everywhere.

- **Function Scope**: `var` variables inside functions are local to those functions.
- **Block Scope**: With `let` and `const`, variables can be scoped to a block.
- **Lexical Scope**: Inner functions can access variables of outer scopes.
- Avoid overusing global variables; keep scopes tight for cleaner, more maintainable code.

Multiple Choice Questions

1. Which of the following has global scope? A. Variables declared with `var` inside a function
B. Variables declared outside any function or block
C. Variables declared with `let` inside a block
D. None of the above
Answer: B
Explanation: Variables declared outside any function or block have global scope.
2. What type of scope did JavaScript have before ES6? A. Function and block scope
B. Global and function scope
C. Block scope only
D. Lexical scope only
Answer: B
Explanation: Before ES6, JavaScript primarily had global and function scope.
3. Variables declared with `let` are: A. Function-scoped
B. Block-scoped
C. Global-scoped only
D. Automatically global

Answer: B

Explanation: `let` is block-scoped.

4. What happens when you reference a `var` variable before it's declared? A. Returns `undefined` due to hoisting

B. Throws a ReferenceError

C. Throws a TypeError

D. Nothing special happens

Answer: A

Explanation: `var` variables are hoisted and initialized as `undefined` if accessed before declaration.

5. What happens when you reference a `let` variable before it's declared? A. Returns `undefined`

B. Throws a ReferenceError

C. Behaves the same as `var`

D. Is automatically assigned a default value

Answer: B

Explanation: `let` variables cannot be accessed before declaration; doing so throws a ReferenceError.

6. Lexical scope means: A. Scope is determined by where variables are called

B. Scope is determined at runtime only

C. Scope is determined by where variables are declared in the source code

D. Scope does not apply to nested functions

Answer: C

Explanation: Lexical scope is determined by the source code structure.

7. Which keyword declares a variable that is function-scoped (in older JavaScript versions)? A. var

B. let

C. const

D. None of the above

Answer: A
Explanation: `var` is function-scoped.
8. Which of the following will be accessible globally if declared at the top-level in a browser environment? A. var topGlobal = 10;
B. let topGlobal = 10;
C. const topGlobal = 10;
D. All of the above are global but only `var` attaches to window.
Answer: D
Explanation: Declaring a variable at the top-level makes it global. However, `var` attaches to `window` in the browser, while `let` and `const` create global variables but do not become properties of the window object in strict mode. Still, they are in global scope.
9. What is variable shadowing? A. When a variable in a nested scope has the same name as one in an outer scope
B. When variables cannot be accessed
C. When global variables disappear
D. When `var` and `let` are used together
Answer: A
Explanation: Variable shadowing occurs when a variable in an inner scope takes precedence over an outer variable with the same name.
10.   In strict mode, what is the default scope of variables if not declared with `var, let,` or `const`? A. Global scope
B. Local scope
C. They cause an error if not declared
D. Automatically assigned to block scope
Answer: C
Explanation: In strict mode, using a variable without declaring it throws a ReferenceError.
11.   `const` variables are: A. Block-scoped
B. Function-scoped

C. Global-scoped only
D. Hoisted as undefined
Answer: A
Explanation: `const` is block-scoped.
12.   The "temporal dead zone" applies to variables declared with: A. var
B. let and const
C. Only const
D. None of the above
Answer: B
Explanation: The temporal dead zone occurs with `let` and `const` before they are declared.
13.   If you have a variable x in the global scope and another x inside a function, when you log x inside the function, which one appears? A. The global x
B. The function's local x (shadowed variable)
C. Both print out
D. Causes an error
Answer: B
Explanation: The local variable x inside the function shadows the global x.
14.   Accessing a global variable inside a function: A. Is not possible in strict mode
B. Is possible unless a local variable with the same name shadows it
C. Always returns undefined
D. Throws an error
Answer: B
Explanation: Global variables are accessible inside functions unless overshadowed by a local variable of the same name.
15.   `var` declarations inside a block (such as an if statement) are: A. Only available inside that block

B. Hoisted to the top of that block only
C. Hoisted to the top of the function or global scope
D. Turned into global variables
Answer: C
Explanation: var is not block-scoped; it hoists to the function or global scope.
16.   Which statement about lexical scope is true? A. Functions only access variables in their own scope
B. Inner functions can access variables in outer functions due to lexical scope
C. Lexical scope is determined at runtime
D. Lexical scope applies only to global variables
Answer: B
Explanation: Inner functions inherit variable access from outer functions due to lexical scope.
17.   IIFEs (Immediately Invoked Function Expressions) are often used to: A. Create global variables
B. Create a local scope to avoid polluting the global scope
C. Remove the need for variables
D. They have no effect on scope
Answer: B
Explanation: IIFEs create a function scope that protects variables from becoming global.
18.   If you declare let i = 0; in a for loop header: A. i is global
B. i is only available inside the loop block
C. i is available after the loop ends
D. i becomes a property of the window object
Answer: B
Explanation: let in a for loop header creates a block-scoped variable visible only inside the loop.
19.   If a function does not explicitly return a variable, where are the variables declared inside it accessible? A. Inside that function only

B. In the global scope

C. In all outer scopes

D. Automatically returned for external use

Answer: A

Explanation: Variables inside a function are not accessible outside unless returned or otherwise exposed.

20. Hoisting means: A. Variables and function declarations are moved to the top of their scope before code execution

B. Variables become block-scoped

C. Functions cannot be called before they are declared

D. Scope rules do not apply

Answer: A

Explanation: Hoisting moves declarations to the top, allowing certain references before actual declaration lines.

10 Coding Exercises with Solutions and Explanations

1. Global vs Local Scope

Problem:
Create a global variable greeting = "Hello". Write a function that declares a local variable name = "Alice" and logs "Hello Alice". Outside the function, log name and explain what happens.

Solution:

```
var greeting = "Hello";
```

```
function sayHello() {
  var name = "Alice";
  console.log(greeting + " " + name); //
"Hello Alice"
}

sayHello();
console.log(typeof name); // "undefined",
because name is local to sayHello.
```

Explanation:
name is function-scoped, so it's not accessible outside the
function.

2. Block Scope with `let`

Problem:
Use an `if` block and declare a variable with `let` inside it.
Attempt to log it outside the block.
Solution:

```
if (true) {
  let blockVar = "I'm block scoped";
  console.log(blockVar); // "I'm block
scoped"
}
// console.log(blockVar); // ReferenceError
```

Explanation:
blockVar is not accessible outside the `if` block.

3. Shadowing Variables

Problem:
Declare a global variable x = 5. Inside a function, declare
a local variable x = 10 and log it. Then log x globally.
Solution:

```
let x = 5;

function test() {
  let x = 10;
  console.log("Inside function: ", x); //
10
}

test();
console.log("Global scope: ", x); // 5
```

Explanation:
The local x shadows the global x inside the function.

4. Hoisting with `var`

Problem:
Log a `var` variable before declaring it, then declare it and
assign a value. Explain the output.
Solution:

```
console.log(myVar); // undefined, due to
hoisting
var myVar = "Hoisted!";
console.log(myVar); // "Hoisted!"
```

Explanation:
var declarations are hoisted and initialized as undefined before assignment.

5. Temporal Dead Zone with `let`

Problem:
Try to access a let variable before it's declared and explain the error.
Solution:

```
// console.log(number); // ReferenceError:
Cannot access 'number' before
initialization
let number = 10;
```

Explanation:
let variables cannot be accessed before their declaration line (temporal dead zone).

6. IIFE to Create Local Scope

Problem:
Use an IIFE to create a local scope and define a variable inside it. Attempt to log that variable outside the IIFE.
Solution:

```
(function() {
  let secret = "I am secret!";
  console.log(secret); // "I am secret!"
})();
```

```
// console.log(secret); // ReferenceError
```

Explanation:
The variable `secret` is not accessible outside the IIFE.

7. Returning Values to Access Variables Outside Function

Problem:
Write a function that declares a `let message = "Hello"` and returns it. Log the returned value outside.
Solution:

```
function getMessage() {
  let message = "Hello";
  return message;
}

let msg = getMessage();
console.log(msg); // "Hello"
```

Explanation:
The `message` variable is local to `getMessage` but returning it lets us use its value outside.

8. Loop Scope with `let`

Problem:
Use a `for` loop with `let i = 0; i < 3; i++`. Log `i` inside and outside the loop.
Solution:

```
for (let i = 0; i < 3; i++) {
   console.log("Inside loop:", i); // 0, 1,
2
}
// console.log(i); // ReferenceError: i not
defined outside the loop
```

Explanation:
i is block-scoped to the loop and not accessible outside it.

9. Lexical Scope Demonstration

Problem:
Create a function outer() that defines a variable let outerVar = "outer". Inside outer(), define another function inner() that logs outerVar. Call inner() from within outer().
Solution:

```
function outer() {
   let outerVar = "outer";
   function inner() {
      console.log(outerVar);
   }
   inner(); // "outer"
}

outer();
```

Explanation:
inner() can access outerVar because of lexical scope.

10. Multiple Scopes Example

Problem:
Declare a global variable `count` = `100`. In a function `resetCount()`, declare a `let` `count` = `0` and log it. Also log the global `count` after calling `resetCount()`.
Solution:

```
let count = 100;

function resetCount() {
  let count = 0;
  console.log("Inside resetCount:", count);
// 0
}

resetCount();
console.log("Global count:", count); // 100
(unchanged)
```

Explanation:
The local `count` in `resetCount` does not affect the global `count`.

Conclusion

Mastering scope in JavaScript is crucial for writing clean, bug-free code. Knowing the differences between global, function, and block scope, and understanding lexical scoping rules, helps avoid variable conflicts and confusing bugs. The introduction of `let` and `const` provides better control over variable lifetimes, while lexical scoping underpins powerful features like closures.

JavaScript Hoisting

Introduction to Hoisting

Hoisting is a mechanism in JavaScript where variable and function declarations are moved to the top of their scope (the global scope or the current function scope) before code execution. This means you can theoretically use variables and functions before they are declared in your code. However, while declarations are hoisted, initializations (assignments) are not. Also, the behavior differs between `var`, `let`, `const` variables, and function declarations vs function expressions.

Key Points:

- Only declarations are hoisted, not assignments.
- `var` variables are hoisted and initialized to `undefined` at the beginning of their scope.
- `let` and `const` variables are hoisted but not initialized, resulting in a "Temporal Dead Zone" if accessed before their declaration.
- Function declarations are hoisted with their entire function body.
- Function expressions and arrow functions assigned to variables behave like variables in terms of hoisting.

Hoisting Variables

Using `var`

Variables declared with `var` are hoisted to the top of their function or global scope and initialized as `undefined`. Accessing them before their declaration will not throw an error, but will yield `undefined`.
Example:

```
console.log(aVar); // undefined, due to
hoisting
var aVar = 10;
console.log(aVar); // 10
```

The actual flow of execution acts like this behind the scenes:

```
var aVar;             // Declarations are
hoisted
console.log(aVar);    // aVar is undefined
aVar = 10;
console.log(aVar);    // 10
```

Using `let` and `const`

`let` and `const` declarations are also hoisted, but unlike `var`, they are not initialized automatically. Instead, they remain in a "Temporal Dead Zone" (TDZ) from the start of the block until the line where they are declared. Accessing them before their declaration results in a ReferenceError.
Example:

```
// console.log(bLet); // ReferenceError:
Cannot access 'bLet' before initialization
```

```
let bLet = 5;
console.log(bLet); // 5
```

Similar for `const`:

```
// console.log(cConst); // ReferenceError
const cConst = 15;
console.log(cConst); // 15
```

Hoisting Functions

Function Declarations

Function declarations are fully hoisted. The entire function is available before it appears in the code.
Example:

```
greet(); // "Hello!"
function greet() {
  console.log("Hello!");
}
```

Under the hood:

```
function greet() { // Declaration is
hoisted
  console.log("Hello!");
}

greet(); // Can call it here safely
```

Function Expressions and Arrow Functions

Function expressions and arrow functions assigned to variables are treated like variables. Only the variable declaration is hoisted, not the function definition.
Example:

```
// sayHi(); // TypeError: sayHi is not a
function

var sayHi = function() {
  console.log("Hi!");
};

sayHi(); // "Hi!"
```

The code above acts like:

```
var sayHi;              // declaration hoisted
// sayHi(); // sayHi is undefined at this
point, cannot call
sayHi = function() {
  console.log("Hi!");
};
sayHi();
```

The same applies to arrow functions:

```
// arrowFunc(); // TypeError: arrowFunc is
not a function
var arrowFunc = () => console.log("Arrow");
arrowFunc(); // "Arrow"
```

Common Pitfalls

1. Using `var` variables before declaring them leads to `undefined`.
2. Using `let` or `const` variables before declaring them causes a ReferenceError due to the temporal dead zone.
3. Calling function expressions or arrow functions before declaring them leads to errors because only the variable is hoisted, not the assignment.

Summary

- **Hoisting** moves declarations to the top of their scope, but assignments stay in place.
- `var` variables get hoisted and initialized to `undefined`.
- `let` and `const` get hoisted but remain uninitialized until their declaration line.
- Function declarations are fully hoisted, allowing them to be called before their declaration.
- Function expressions and arrow functions are treated like variables and are not fully hoisted.

Multiple Choice Questions (With Answers and Explanations)

1. What is hoisting in JavaScript? A. Moving declarations and initializations to the bottom of the code
B. Moving only initializations to the top of the code
C. Moving declarations to the top of their scope before code execution
D. Not a concept in JavaScript

Answer: C

Explanation: Hoisting is the process of moving declarations to the top of their scope.

2. Which of the following are fully hoisted in JavaScript?

A. var variables

B. let variables

C. Function declarations

D. Arrow functions

Answer: C

Explanation: Function declarations are fully hoisted with their definitions.

3. What will `console.log(x); var x = 10;` output?

A. 10

B. undefined

C. ReferenceError

D. null

Answer: B

Explanation: `var` x is hoisted, so x exists but is undefined at the time of logging.

4. What happens if you reference a `let` variable before its declaration? A. Returns undefined

B. Throws a ReferenceError

C. Throws a TypeError

D. It logs 0 by default

Answer: B

Explanation: Accessing a `let` variable before declaration is a ReferenceError.

5. Which of these statements about `const` variables and hoisting is true? A. const variables are not hoisted at all

B. const variables are hoisted but not initialized

C. const variables are hoisted and assigned undefined by default

D. const variables can be accessed before declaration safely

Answer: B
Explanation: `const` variables are hoisted but remain uninitialized until the declaration line.
6. Function expressions are hoisted as: A. Fully defined functions
B. Variables set to undefined
C. Not hoisted at all
D. Arrow functions
Answer: B
Explanation: Function expressions are hoisted like variables, so the variable is defined as `undefined` until the assignment.
7. If you call a function declared as `function greet()` `{...}` before its definition, what happens? A. It works, because function declarations are hoisted
B. ReferenceError
C. TypeError
D. Returns undefined
Answer: A
Explanation: Function declarations are hoisted completely, so you can call them before they appear.
8. The "temporal dead zone" refers to: A. The time between starting the script and first variable declaration
B. The area in code where `let` and `const` variables exist but are not initialized
C. A runtime error that occurs at midnight
D. A region in global scope inaccessible to functions
Answer: B
Explanation: The temporal dead zone is the time between hoisting and declaration where `let` and `const` variables cannot be accessed.
What does the following log?
```
console.log(typeof greet);
function greet() {}
```

9. A. "function"
B. "undefined"
C. ReferenceError
D. TypeError
Answer: A
Explanation: Function declarations are hoisted, so `typeof greet` is "function" even before the definition line.
10.   Which keyword(s) do not initialize variables as `undefined` at the start of their scope? A. var
B. let and const
C. function
D. All keywords initialize variables
Answer: B
Explanation: `let` and `const` are hoisted but not initialized, causing a ReferenceError if accessed prematurely.
Consider:
```
console.log(myVar);
let myVar = 20;
```
11.   What is the result? A. undefined
B. 20
C. ReferenceError
D. null
Answer: C
Explanation: `let myVar` is in the temporal dead zone until its declaration line.
12.   Arrow functions assigned to a `var` variable are hoisted as: A. Fully functional arrow functions
B. Undefined variables
C. Function declarations
D. Immutable constants
Answer: B

Explanation: Like function expressions, arrow functions assigned to `var` are hoisted as undefined variables.

13.   Which statement is true about hoisting `var` variables?
A. They are not hoisted at all
B. They are hoisted and initialized to `undefined`
C. They cause a ReferenceError if used before declaration
D. They are hoisted but immediately throw a TypeError when accessed

Answer: B

Explanation: `var` variables are hoisted and initialized to undefined.

14.   Which scenario causes a ReferenceError due to hoisting and variable initialization rules? A. Using a function declaration before defining it
B. Using a `var` variable before declaration
C. Using a `let` variable before declaration
D. Calling a fully hoisted function declaration after definition

Answer: C

Explanation: Accessing `let` before its declaration throws a ReferenceError.

15.   Which of the following will not throw an error when called before its definition? A. Function declaration
B. Function expression assigned to a `var`
C. Arrow function assigned to a `var`
D. Using `let` variable before declaration

Answer: A

Explanation: Only function declarations are safe to call before definition.

16.   In which order does hoisting occur? A. Variables are hoisted after the code executes
B. Functions and variables are hoisted before the code executes
C. Only variables are hoisted, functions are not

D. Hoisting does not occur in modern JavaScript
Answer: B
Explanation: All declarations are hoisted before code execution.
Consider:
```
console.log(a);
var a = 10;
```
17. This logs: A. undefined
B. 10
C. ReferenceError
D. null
Answer: A
Explanation: `var a` is hoisted and initialized with undefined, so it logs undefined first.
18. Which variable declaration is most likely to cause confusion if relied on due to hoisting? A. let x = 5;
B. const y = 10;
C. var z = 15;
D. function foo() {}
Answer: C
Explanation: `var` hoisting often causes confusion because it initializes to undefined and doesn't throw errors.
19. When are `const` variables initialized? A. At the top of their scope, just like var
B. At the point of their declaration in code
C. They are never initialized
D. After code execution completes
Answer: B
Explanation: `const` variables are initialized at their declaration line, not before.
20. If you rely on hoisting for logic, what is a best practice? A. Avoid relying on hoisting; always declare variables before use

B. Always use `var` to ensure initialization

C. Always call functions before they are defined

D. Never use `let` or `const`

Answer: A

Explanation: Best practice is to write code as if hoisting doesn't exist to avoid confusion.

10 Coding Exercises with Solutions and Explanations

1. Hoisting with `var`

Problem:
Write code that uses a `var` variable before it is declared. Print it out before and after the declaration. Explain the output.

Solution:

```
console.log(myVar); // undefined due to
hoisting
var myVar = 100;
console.log(myVar); // 100
```

Explanation:
`myVar` is hoisted as `undefined`, so the first log shows `undefined`. After assignment, it shows `100`.

2. Hoisting with `let` (Temporal Dead Zone)

Problem:
Try to print a `let` variable before its declaration and handle the error.
Solution:

```
// console.log(myLet); // ReferenceError:
Cannot access 'myLet' before initialization
let myLet = 5;
console.log(myLet); // 5
```

Explanation:
`myLet` is in the temporal dead zone before its declaration line.

3. Function Declaration Hoisting

Problem:
Call a function declaration before it's defined and verify it works.
Solution:

```
greet(); // "Hello!"

function greet() {
  console.log("Hello!");
}
```

Explanation:
Function declarations are fully hoisted, so we can call `greet()` before defining it.

4. Function Expression Hoisting

Problem:
Try to call a function expression before it's defined and explain the error.
Solution:

```
// sayHello(); // TypeError: sayHello is
not a function
var sayHello = function() {
  console.log("Hello!");
};

sayHello(); // Works here: "Hello!"
```

Explanation:
var sayHello is hoisted as undefined. Calling it before assignment leads to a TypeError.

5. Arrow Function Hoisting

Problem:
Write an arrow function assigned to a var variable and call it before and after definition.
Solution:

```
// arrowFn(); // TypeError: arrowFn is not
a function
var arrowFn = () => console.log("Arrow");
arrowFn(); // "Arrow"
```

Explanation:
Like function expressions, arrow functions are hoisted as undefined variables.

6. Multiple `var` Declarations

Problem:
Declare a `var` variable multiple times in the same scope and log its value before and after assignments.
Solution:

```
console.log(testVar); // undefined
var testVar = 1;
var testVar = 2; // Allowed with var
console.log(testVar); // 2
```

Explanation:
All `var` declarations are hoisted. The variable is `undefined` initially, then reassigned to 1, then 2.

7. Hoisting with Nested Functions

Problem:
Write a function that calls an inner function before its declaration inside the same outer function.
Solution:

```
function outer() {
  inner(); // "Inner function"
  function inner() {
    console.log("Inner function");
```

```
    }
}

outer();
```

Explanation:
Inner function declarations are hoisted to the top of `outer`'s scope.

8. Hoisting a `const` Variable

Problem:
Attempt to log a `const` variable before declaration.
Solution:

```
// console.log(PI); // ReferenceError
const PI = 3.14;
console.log(PI); // 3.14
```

Explanation:
`PI` is hoisted but not initialized, causing a ReferenceError if accessed prematurely.

9. Conditional Hoisting

Problem:
Declare a function inside an if statement using a function declaration. Call the function outside the if statement.
Solution:

```
if (true) {
    function conditionalFunc() {
```

```
        return "Condition met";
    }
}

console.log(conditionalFunc()); //
"Condition met" (in non-strict mode,
function declarations inside blocks are
hoisted to either global or function scope
depending on environment)
```

Explanation:
Function declarations inside blocks are subject to
environment-specific behavior. In strict mode, block-level
function declarations are not accessible outside the block.
In loose mode (older browsers), they may still be hoisted to
the enclosing scope. This can vary, so best practice is not to
rely on this.

10. Preventing Hoisting Issues

Problem:
Rearrange the following code so it runs without errors,
avoiding reliance on hoisting:

```
// Original (error):
// console.log(msg);
// let msg = "Fixed!";
```

Solution:

```
let msg = "Fixed!";
console.log(msg); // "Fixed!"
```

Explanation:
By declaring `msg` before use, we avoid the ReferenceError caused by the temporal dead zone.

Conclusion

Hoisting is a fundamental JavaScript behavior that can surprise beginners. Understanding that declarations (both variables and functions) are moved to the top of their scope before code execution is crucial. With `var`, you get undefined values if you access variables too early, while `let` and `const` trigger ReferenceErrors due to the temporal dead zone. Function declarations are safe to call before they appear, but function expressions and arrow functions are not.

By practicing the exercises and reviewing the multiple-choice questions, you should now have a solid grasp of how hoisting works in JavaScript and how to write cleaner, more predictable code.

JavaScript Closures

Introduction

Closures are a fundamental concept in JavaScript. Understanding them is crucial for mastering advanced topics, such as data privacy, encapsulation, and functional programming patterns. A closure gives you access to an outer function's scope from within an inner function, even after the outer function has returned.

What is a Closure?

A **closure** is formed when an inner function captures variables from its outer (enclosing) scope. Even if the outer function returns or finishes execution, the inner function can still access these variables. This happens because JavaScript uses **lexical scoping** and maintains a reference to the outer function's environment.

Key points about closures:
- They are created at function creation time, not at execution time.
- The inner function retains access to variables in the outer function's scope chain.
- Variables captured by a closure are kept "alive" as long as the closure exists.

How Closures Work

Consider the following example:

```
function outer() {
  let count = 0;
  function inner() {
    count++;
    console.log(count);
  }
  return inner;
}

const counter = outer();
```

```
counter(); // 1
counter(); // 2
counter(); // 3
```

Explanation:
- `outer()` defines a local variable `count` and returns the inner function `inner`.
- When `outer()` is called, it returns `inner`, and `outer()`'s execution context ends.
- However, the returned function `inner` still has access to `count` because of the closure.
- Each call to `counter()` increments and logs `count`. Closures enable the inner function to "remember" the environment in which it was created.

Common Use Cases of Closures

Data Privacy and Encapsulation:
Closures can be used to keep variables private and only accessible through privileged functions.

```
function createCounter() {
  let count = 0;
  return {
    increment: function() { count++; },
    getValue: function() { return count; }
  };
}

const c = createCounter();
c.increment();
console.log(c.getValue()); // 1
1.
```

Partial Application and Currying:
Closures can store parameters for later use.

```
function add(a) {
  return function(b) {
    return a + b; // closure stores 'a'
  };
}

const add5 = add(5);
console.log(add5(10)); // 15
```

2.

3. **Event Handlers and Asynchronous Code:**
Closures are used when callbacks retain access to variables of a function that has already completed execution.

Closures and Garbage Collection

Closures keep variables in memory as long as the closure exists. If not managed properly, this can lead to increased memory usage. However, as soon as there are no references to the closure function, the variables can be garbage-collected.

Best Practices

- Use closures intentionally to maintain state and encapsulate data.
- Be mindful of memory usage and avoid unnecessary closures.
- Understand that closures capture variables, not just values at the time of creation.

Multiple Choice Questions (With Answers and Explanations)

1. What is a closure in JavaScript?
A. A feature that prevents accessing variables from outer scopes
B. An inner function that has access to variables in its outer function's scope, even after the outer function has returned
C. A method of compiling code for better performance
D. A memory management technique
Answer: B
Explanation: Closures allow an inner function to access outer scope variables even after the outer function finishes execution.

2. In a closure, where are the outer variables stored after the outer function returns?
A. They are discarded immediately
B. They are stored on the global object
C. They remain in the inner function's lexical environment
D. They move into localStorage
Answer: C
Explanation: The inner function keeps a reference to its lexical environment, preserving outer variables.

Which of the following demonstrates a closure?

```
function outer() {
  let x = 10;
  function inner() {
    console.log(x);
  }
  return inner;
}
```

```
const fn = outer();
fn();
```
3. A. No closure is formed

B. A closure is formed when fn is returned and called later

C. Closure is formed only if x is a global variable

D. Closure is formed only if x is passed as an argument

Answer: B

Explanation: `fn` is a closure that retains access to `x` after `outer()` returns.

4. Closures are related to which type of scoping? A. Dynamic scoping

B. Lexical scoping

C. Block scoping only

D. Global scoping

Answer: B

Explanation: JavaScript uses lexical scoping, which is key to how closures work.

5. What is retained by the closure? A. A copy of the variable's value at creation time

B. A reference to the variable's memory location, allowing updates

C. Only primitive values but not objects

D. Nothing is retained

Answer: B

Explanation: Closures keep references to variables, not just copies of their values.

6. Can a closure access variables in the global scope? A. No, closures only access outer function scope

B. Yes, closures can access any scope they are lexically nested within, including global

C. Only if the variable is declared with var

D. Only if strict mode is disabled

Answer: B

Explanation: Closures can access the global scope and any other outer scopes as per lexical scoping.

7. Which pattern uses closures for data privacy? A. The module pattern

B. The singleton pattern

C. The factory pattern

D. The observer pattern

Answer: A

Explanation: The module pattern commonly uses closures for private state.

If we have:

```
function makeAdder(a) {
   return function(b) {
      return a + b;
   };
}
let add10 = makeAdder(10);
console.log(add10(5));
```

8. What is logged? A. 5

B. 10

C. 15

D. ReferenceError

Answer: C

Explanation: `makeAdder` returns a closure that keeps `a=10`, so `add10(5)` returns 15.

9. Closures can lead to memory leaks if: A. They never happen in JavaScript

B. References to them persist and keep large objects in memory

C. They are used with arrow functions only

D. They are explicitly deleted

Answer: B

Explanation: If a closure references large data and remains accessible, it can prevent garbage collection.

10. Are closures created at the time of: A. Function creation
B. Function execution
C. When garbage collection runs
D. When the variables are mutated
Answer: A
Explanation: Closures form when the function is created, not when it's executed.
11. Does returning an inner function from an outer function always create a closure? A. Yes, if the inner function uses variables from the outer function's scope
B. No, never
C. Only if `var` is used
D. Only if `use strict` is enabled
Answer: A
Explanation: Returning an inner function that references outer variables creates a closure.
12. Can a closure outlive its outer function? A. No, once outer function returns, variables are gone
B. Yes, if a reference to the inner function is kept
C. Only in older browsers
D. Only with ES6 features
Answer: B
Explanation: The inner function's closure keeps outer variables alive as long as the inner function exists.
In the following code:

```
for (var i=0; i<3; i++) {
  setTimeout(function() {
    console.log(i);
  }, 100);
}
```

13.   What gets logged? A. 0, 1, 2

B. 3, 3, 3

C. It depends on the environment

D. Error

Answer: B

Explanation: Due to closure with `var`, all timeouts use the final value of i (which is 3). Using `let` would fix this.

14.   Which concept allows closures to "remember" the context? A. Prototypal inheritance

B. Lexical environment

C. The event loop

D. JSON parsing

Answer: B

Explanation: The lexical environment is what stores variable references and allows closures to remember context.

15.   Are closures unique to JavaScript? A. Yes, only JavaScript has closures

B. No, many languages implement closures

C. Closures are not real, just a theory

D. Only Node.js supports closures

Answer: B

Explanation: Closures exist in many programming languages, not just JavaScript.

16.   When might you want to use a closure? A. To hide implementation details and provide a controlled interface

B. Never, closures are bad practice

C. Only for asynchronous code

D. Only in frameworks, not in vanilla JavaScript

Answer: A

Explanation: Closures are great for encapsulation and controlling variable access.

17.   Can closures capture dynamically changing variables? A. No, once captured the value never changes

B. Yes, they capture references, so if the variable changes

later, closure sees the updated value
C. Only primitives can change
D. Only if using `const`
Answer: B
Explanation: Since closures hold references, if the variable changes, the closure will access the updated value.
18.   If a closure needs to preserve a private variable and provide methods to manipulate it, which pattern is often used? A. Revealing module pattern
B. Singleton pattern
C. Constructor pattern
D. Adapter pattern
Answer: A
Explanation: The revealing module pattern uses closures to expose methods while hiding private data.
19.   In strict mode, do closures still work the same way?
A. No, closures are disabled in strict mode
B. Yes, closures work the same way
C. Closures throw errors in strict mode
D. Variables are not accessible at all in strict mode
Answer: B
Explanation: Strict mode does not change how closures work.
20.   Is it possible to have multiple closures referencing the same outer scope variables? A. No, only one closure can reference a given variable
B. Yes, multiple closures can form over the same scope and all share those variables
C. Each closure gets its own copy of variables
D. It depends on the browser
Answer: B
Explanation: Multiple closures can share the same variables if they originate from the same outer scope.

10 Coding Exercises with Solutions and Explanations

1. Basic Closure

Problem:
Write a function `makeCounter` that returns a function that increments and logs a private counter variable each time it's called.

Solution:

```
function makeCounter() {
  let count = 0;
  return function() {
    count++;
    console.log(count);
  };
}

const counter = makeCounter();
counter(); // 1
counter(); // 2
counter(); // 3
```

Explanation:
`count` is private to `makeCounter`. The returned function forms a closure and maintains access to `count`.

2. Private Data with Closures

Problem:
Create a function `createPerson` that takes a `name` parameter and returns two functions: one to get the name and one to set a new name. Keep `name` private.
Solution:

```
function createPerson(name) {
  return {
    getName: function() { return name; },
    setName: function(newName) { name =
newName; }
  };
}


const person = createPerson("Alice");
console.log(person.getName()); // "Alice"
person.setName("Bob");
console.log(person.getName()); // "Bob"
```

Explanation:
The variable `name` is hidden inside `createPerson`. The returned methods form closures that access `name`.

3. Using Closures to Implement Partial Application

Problem:
Write a function `add(a)` that returns a function which takes `b` and returns `a + b`.
Solution:

```
function add(a) {
```

```
  return function(b) {
    return a + b;
  };
}

const add10 = add(10);
console.log(add10(5)); // 15
```

Explanation:
add(10) returns a closure that remembers a=10. When
called with 5, it returns 15.

4. Closures in Loops (Fixing var Issue)

Problem:
Print the numbers 0, 1, 2 with a delay using setTimeout.
Use closures to ensure each callback remembers the correct
i.
Solution:

```
for (var i = 0; i < 3; i++) {
  (function(j) {
    setTimeout(function() {
      console.log(j);
    }, 100);
  })(i);
}
```

Explanation:
An IIFE captures i as j in each iteration, creating a closure
that stores the correct value.

5. Returning Objects That Use Closure

Problem:
Create a bankAccount function that returns an object
with methods deposit, withdraw, and getBalance.
Keep balance private.
Solution:

```
function bankAccount(initialBalance) {
  let balance = initialBalance;
  return {
    deposit: amount => balance += amount,
    withdraw: amount => balance -= amount,
    getBalance: () => balance
  };
}
```

```
const account = bankAccount(100);
account.deposit(50);
console.log(account.getBalance()); // 150
account.withdraw(20);
console.log(account.getBalance()); // 130
```

Explanation:
balance is private. The methods form closures that access
and modify balance.

6. Closures and Event Listeners

Problem (conceptual):
Create a click handler that remembers a count of how

many times a button is clicked, without using any global variables.
Solution:

```
function createClickHandler() {
  let count = 0;
  return function() {
    count++;
    console.log("Clicked " + count + "
times");
  };
}

const button =
document.createElement("button");
button.textContent = "Click me";
document.body.appendChild(button);

const handler = createClickHandler();
button.addEventListener("click", handler);
```

Explanation:
handler forms a closure over count. Each click updates and logs it.

7. Closure for Configuration

Problem:
Create a configureGreeting(prefix) function that returns a function that takes a name and prints prefix + name.
Solution:

```
function configureGreeting(prefix) {
  return function(name) {
    console.log(prefix + " " + name);
  };
}
```

```
const greetHello =
configureGreeting("Hello");
greetHello("Alice"); // "Hello Alice"
```

Explanation:
The returned function closes over `prefix`.

8. Closure with Timer

Problem:
Use a closure to create a timer function
`startTimer(duration)` that logs every second until
duration is reached.
Solution:

```
function startTimer(duration) {
  let timeLeft = duration;
  let interval = setInterval(function() {
    console.log(timeLeft);
    timeLeft--;
    if (timeLeft < 0) {
      clearInterval(interval);
    }
  }, 1000);
}
```

```
startTimer(3); // logs 3, then 2, then 1,
then 0
```

Explanation:
The anonymous function inside `setInterval` is a closure
capturing `timeLeft`.

9. Memory and Closures

Problem:
Create a closure that stores a large array and logs its length
when called. Ensure the array isn't garbage-collected.
Solution:

```
function storeLargeData() {
   let largeArray = new
Array(1000000).fill(0);
   return function() {
     console.log("Array length:",
largeArray.length);
   };
}

const logData = storeLargeData();
logData(); // "Array length: 1000000"
```

Explanation:
`largeArray` remains in memory due to the closure, so
calling `logData()` shows the large array is still accessible.

10. Multiple Closures Sharing the Same Scope

Problem:
Create two closures from the same outer function that increment and decrement the same private counter.
Solution:

```
function createCounter() {
  let value = 0;
  return {
    increment: function() { value++;
console.log(value); },
    decrement: function() { value--;
console.log(value); }
  };
}

const c = createCounter();
c.increment(); // 1
c.increment(); // 2
c.decrement(); // 1
```

Explanation:
Both `increment` and `decrement` share the same `value` variable, demonstrating multiple closures over the same scope.

Conclusion

Closures are a powerful feature of JavaScript, leveraging lexical scoping to preserve access to variables of an outer function from an inner function. They enable data encapsulation, stateful functions, and more expressive code patterns. By understanding closures, you unlock advanced techniques in functional programming, event handling, and module patterns, making your code more modular, maintainable, and flexible.

JavaScript Callbacks

Introduction

A **callback** is a function passed as an argument to another function to be executed later. Callbacks are fundamental to JavaScript, allowing you to control the flow of functions, handle events, and work with asynchronous operations. Understanding callbacks is key to writing clean, maintainable code, especially when dealing with operations that take time, such as network requests or file I/O.

Synchronous vs Asynchronous Callbacks

Synchronous Callback:
A synchronous callback is executed right away, as part of the main execution flow. The callback function runs immediately within the function it's passed to, blocking further code execution until it returns.
Example of a Synchronous Callback:

```
function greet(name, callback) {
  callback("Hello, " + name);
}
```

```
greet("Alice", function(message) {
  console.log(message); // "Hello, Alice"
});
// The callback runs immediately during the
execution of `greet`
```

Key points about synchronous callbacks:
- They run in the same call stack.
- They do not cause delays or require waiting.
- Useful for tasks that do not block the main thread or are meant to run immediately.

Asynchronous Callback:
An asynchronous callback is executed at a later time, typically after an asynchronous operation completes (e.g., fetching data from a server, reading a file, or using timers).

Example of an Asynchronous Callback:

```
console.log("Start");

setTimeout(function() {
  console.log("Asynchronous callback
executed");
}, 1000);

console.log("End");
```

Key points about asynchronous callbacks:
- They do not run immediately; they are deferred until a certain event completes.
- They often involve working with the event loop and concurrency model of JavaScript.

- Commonly used in network requests, file reads, event handling, and timeouts.

The Event Loop and Callbacks

JavaScript runs on a single thread but uses an event loop to handle asynchronous callbacks. When an async function finishes (like a network request), the callback is queued and will run after the current stack is empty.

Common Use Cases of Callbacks

Event Handling:
DOM events, such as `click` or `keydown`, often require callbacks.
```
document.querySelector("button").addEventLi
stener("click", function() {
  console.log("Button clicked!");
});
```
1.
Timers: `setTimeout` and `setInterval` use callbacks to execute code after a delay.
```
setTimeout(() => console.log("Done
waiting!"), 2000);
```
2.
Async Operations (e.g., AJAX calls): Using older APIs like `XMLHttpRequest`:
```
const xhr = new XMLHttpRequest();
xhr.open("GET", "data.json");
xhr.onload = function() {
  console.log("Response received",
xhr.response);
```

```
};
xhr.send();
```
3.

Array Methods: Higher-order array methods like `map`, `filter,` and `forEach` accept synchronous callbacks.
```
[1,2,3].forEach(function(num) {
  console.log(num);
});
```
4.

Handling Callback Hell

Callback hell refers to the situation where multiple asynchronous operations are chained, causing deeply nested callbacks, making code hard to read and maintain.
Example of Callback Hell:

```
getData(function(data) {
  processData(data, function(processed) {
    saveData(processed, function(saved) {
      console.log("Data saved!");
    });
  });
});
```

Avoiding Callback Hell:
- Use Promises or async/await to write more readable asynchronous code.
- Modularize code into separate functions.
- Handle errors carefully.

Error-First Callbacks

In Node.js and many asynchronous APIs, callbacks follow an **error-first** style. The first argument to the callback is an error (if any), followed by the result.
Example:

```
function readFile(filePath, callback) {
  // Simulate async file read
  setTimeout(function() {
    let err = null;
    let data = "File content";
    // if an error occurred, err = new
Error("Could not read file");
    callback(err, data);
  }, 1000);
}

readFile("myfile.txt", function(err, data)
{
  if (err) {
    console.error("Error reading file:",
err);
  } else {
    console.log("File data:", data);
  }
});
```

Multiple Choice Questions (With Answers and Explanations)

1. What is a callback in JavaScript? A. A function that runs automatically at the start of a script

B. A function passed to another function to be called later

C. A new type of variable

D. A reserved keyword

Answer: B

Explanation: Callbacks are functions passed as arguments to be executed later.

2. Which of the following is an example of a synchronous callback? A. `setTimeout(() => {...}, 1000)`

B. Event listener callbacks

C. `array.forEach(item => console.log(item))`

D. AJAX request callbacks

Answer: C

Explanation: `forEach` runs immediately and synchronously.

3. What best describes asynchronous callbacks? A. They run immediately, blocking the main thread

B. They execute only after their parent function returns a value

C. They are scheduled to run after an asynchronous operation completes

D. They never run in JavaScript

Answer: C

Explanation: Asynchronous callbacks run after an async operation finishes.

4. The term "callback hell" refers to: A. Errors that occur when using callbacks incorrectly

B. Deeply nested callbacks that reduce code readability

C. A special debugging mode for callbacks

D. The global namespace for callbacks

Answer: B

Explanation: Callback hell is when callbacks are nested to multiple levels, making code hard to read.

5. Which mechanism manages the execution order of asynchronous callbacks in JavaScript? A. The call stack only

B. The event loop and callback queue

C. The GPU pipeline

D. The global object

Answer: B

Explanation: The event loop and callback queue handle asynchronous callback execution.

6. Which is not a common use case for asynchronous callbacks? A. Handling user input events

B. Performing immediate arithmetic operations

C. Making network requests

D. Reading files from disk

Answer: B

Explanation: Simple arithmetic is synchronous and immediate, no callback needed.

7. In Node.js, the error-first callback convention means: A. The callback must always throw an error first

B. The callback first argument is an error object or null

C. The callback must return a Promise

D. The callback cannot return any values

Answer: B

Explanation: Error-first callbacks have the signature `function(err, result)`.

8. Synchronous callbacks are executed: A. After a delay

B. On the next tick of the event loop

C. As soon as the function receiving the callback invokes it

D. Never

Answer: C

Explanation: Synchronous callbacks run immediately within the function's execution.

9. `setTimeout` uses which type of callback? A. Synchronous callback
B. Asynchronous callback
C. Error-first callback
D. No callback at all
Answer: B
Explanation: `setTimeout` schedules code to run later, hence asynchronous.
10.　How can callback hell be mitigated? A. Using more callbacks
B. Using promises or async/await
C. Using synchronous operations only
D. Ignoring errors
Answer: B
Explanation: Promises and async/await help flatten nested callbacks.
11.　`addEventListener('click', () => {})` is an example of: A. Synchronous callback
B. Asynchronous callback triggered by an event
C. Error-first callback
D. A promise
Answer: B
Explanation: The callback runs when the event occurs, which is asynchronous.
12.　If you pass a function as an argument to `anotherFunction`, this function is known as: A. Higher-order function
B. Callback function
C. Constructor function
D. IIFE
Answer: B
Explanation: A function passed as an argument is a callback.

13.   Callback functions in array methods like `map` and `filter` are: A. Always asynchronous

B. Always synchronous

C. Always error-first

D. Dependent on the environment

Answer: B

Explanation: `map` and `filter` callbacks run synchronously as part of array processing.

14.   In a Node.js style callback: `function(err, data)` `{}`, what does `err` represent? A. Always an Error object

B. Either null or an Error object if something went wrong

C. The data returned by the operation

D. It's never used

Answer: B

Explanation: `err` is null if no error, otherwise it's an error object.

15.   The primary reason JavaScript relies on callbacks for asynchronous operations is: A. JavaScript is multi-threaded

B. JavaScript has a single-threaded, non-blocking event loop model

C. JavaScript is compiled

D. JavaScript cannot handle synchronous code

Answer: B

Explanation: The single-threaded event loop model necessitates callbacks for non-blocking async tasks.

16.   `requestAnimationFrame(callback)` executes the callback: A. Immediately

B. After a specified delay

C. On the next browser repaint cycle

D. Never

Answer: C

Explanation: `requestAnimationFrame` schedules the callback before the next repaint.

17.   Which is true about asynchronous callbacks and the main thread? A. They block the main thread until completion

B. They run concurrently on a separate thread

C. They are queued and executed after current code completes

D. They run before the current code finishes

Answer: C

Explanation: Async callbacks are queued and run later, not blocking the main thread.

18.   An error-first callback pattern typically looks like: A. `(err) => { ... }`

B. `(data) => { ... }`

C. `(err, data) => { ... }`

D. `(data, err) => { ... }`

Answer: C

Explanation: Error-first callbacks are usually `(err, data)`.

19.   If a callback is never called: A. The code might hang, waiting for it

B. Nothing else can ever run

C. It's fine, no issues

D. It might cause a memory leak or unhandled scenario

Answer: D

Explanation: If a callback is expected but not called, it may lead to unhandled states or memory issues.

20.   Asynchronous callbacks improve: A. Code simplicity

B. Responsiveness of applications by not blocking the main thread

C. The need for error handling

D. Memory usage

Answer: B

Explanation: Asynchronous callbacks keep the app responsive by not blocking the main thread.

10 Coding Exercises with Solutions and Explanations

1. Synchronous Callback Example

Problem:
Write a function `processArray(arr, callback)` that applies `callback` to each element of `arr` and logs the result.
Solution:

```
function processArray(arr, callback) {
  for (let i = 0; i < arr.length; i++) {
    console.log(callback(arr[i]));
  }
}

processArray([1,2,3], function(num) {
  return num * 2;
});
// Logs: 2, 4, 6
```

Explanation:
Here, `callback` runs synchronously for each array element.

2. Asynchronous Timeout Callback

Problem:
Use `setTimeout` to log "Hello, Async!" after 1 second.
Solution:

```
setTimeout(() => {
  console.log("Hello, Async!");
}, 1000);
```

Explanation:
The callback is asynchronous, executed after the timeout.

3. Reading Data with Callbacks (Simulated)

Problem:
Write a function `getData(callback)` that after 500ms
calls `callback` with a simulated data object.
Solution:

```
function getData(callback) {
  setTimeout(() => {
    callback({ name: "Alice", age: 25 });
  }, 500);
}

getData(function(data) {
  console.log("Received:", data);
});
```

Explanation:
The callback runs after the async timeout completes.

4. Error-First Callback Simulation

Problem:
Write `simulateReadFile(fileName, callback)` that after 300ms, calls `callback(null, "File Content")` if `fileName` is "valid.txt", otherwise `callback(new Error("File not found"))`.
Solution:

```
function simulateReadFile(fileName,
callback) {
  setTimeout(() => {
    if (fileName === "valid.txt") {
      callback(null, "File Content");
    } else {
      callback(new Error("File not
found"));
    }
  }, 300);
}

simulateReadFile("valid.txt", (err, data)
=> {
  if (err) console.error(err);
  else console.log(data); // "File Content"
});
```

Explanation:
Uses the error-first pattern. If an error occurs, pass `err` as the first argument.

5. Avoiding Callback Hell (Refactoring)

144

Problem:
We have nested callbacks:

```javascript
getUser(function(user) {
  getOrders(user, function(orders) {
    getOrderDetails(orders[0],
function(details) {
      console.log(details);
    });
  });
});
```

Refactor into separate named functions.
Solution:

```javascript
function handleDetails(details) {
  console.log(details);
}

function handleOrders(orders) {
  getOrderDetails(orders[0],
handleDetails);
}

function handleUser(user) {
  getOrders(user, handleOrders);
}

getUser(handleUser);
```

Explanation:
By using named functions, the code is more readable and avoids deep nesting.
(Note: `getUser`, `getOrders`, and `getOrderDetails` are assumed predefined functions.)

6. Asynchronous Event Callback

Problem:
Set up a click event on a button that logs "Button clicked!" when pressed.
Solution:

```
const button =
document.createElement("button");
button.textContent = "Click me";
document.body.appendChild(button);

button.addEventListener("click", () => {
  console.log("Button clicked!");
});
```

Explanation:
The callback runs only when the button is clicked (asynchronous event).

7. Using Callbacks with Array Methods

Problem:
Use map with a callback to create a new array that doubles each element of [2,4,6].
Solution:

```
const doubled = [2,4,6].map(function(num) {
    return num * 2;
});
console.log(doubled); // [4,8,12]
```

Explanation:
map uses a synchronous callback, immediately processing each element.

8. Creating a Delayed Execution with Callbacks

Problem:
Write delayLog(message, time, callback) that
waits time ms, logs message, then calls callback().
Solution:

```
function delayLog(message, time, callback)
{
    setTimeout(() => {
        console.log(message);
        callback();
    }, time);
}

delayLog("Waited 1 second", 1000, () => {
    console.log("Callback after message");
});
```

Explanation:
After logging the message, we call the callback to signal completion.

9. Sequential Async Callbacks

Problem:
Call `getData` twice in a sequence (from exercise 3). First fetch `data1`, then once done, fetch `data2` using callbacks.
Solution:

```
function getData(callback) {
  setTimeout(() => {
    callback({value: Math.random()});
  }, 500);
}

getData(function(data1) {
  console.log("Data1:", data1);
  getData(function(data2) {
    console.log("Data2:", data2);
  });
});
```

Explanation:
The second `getData` call is inside the callback of the first, ensuring sequential execution.

10. Implementing Your Own ForEach with Callbacks

Problem:
Write a function `myForEach(arr, callback)` that imitates the behavior of the built-in `forEach`.
Solution:

```
function myForEach(arr, callback) {
  for (let i = 0; i < arr.length; i++) {
    callback(arr[i], i, arr);
  }
}

myForEach([10,20,30], (item, index) => {
  console.log(`Index ${index}: ${item}`);
});
// Logs:
// Index 0: 10
// Index 1: 20
// Index 2: 30
```

Explanation:
myForEach calls the callback for each element, just like the native forEach method.

Conclusion

Callbacks are essential in JavaScript for handling asynchronous operations, event-driven code, and controlling execution order. Understanding the difference between synchronous and asynchronous callbacks, the event loop, and best practices (like error-first callbacks) will help you write efficient, maintainable code. While callbacks can sometimes lead to "callback hell," modern features such as promises and async/await make asynchronous code more readable and manageable.

By mastering callbacks, you gain a strong foundation for building complex, responsive, and non-blocking JavaScript applications.

JavaScript Promises

Introduction

A **Promise** in JavaScript is an object that represents the eventual completion (or failure) of an asynchronous operation and its resulting value. Instead of dealing with nested callbacks (callback hell), Promises provide a cleaner, more maintainable way to handle asynchronous code. A Promise can be in one of three states:

1. **Pending**: The initial state; the operation has not yet completed.
2. **Fulfilled**: The operation completed successfully, and the promise now has a value.
3. **Rejected**: The operation failed, and the promise now has a reason for its failure.

Once a promise is fulfilled or rejected, it becomes settled, and its state cannot change again.

Creating a Promise

You can create a promise using the `new Promise` constructor, which takes an executor function with two arguments: `resolve` and `reject`.

Example:

```
const myPromise = new Promise((resolve,
reject) => {
```

```
  // Perform some async operation
  setTimeout(() => {
    // For example, if the operation is
successful
    resolve("Data received");
  }, 1000);
});
```

Key points:
• Call `resolve(value)` to fulfill the promise with a value.
• Call `reject(reason)` to reject the promise with a reason (usually an error).

Consuming a Promise

You can consume a promise by using the `.then()` and `.catch()` methods:
• **then(onFulfilled, onRejected?)**: Attaches callbacks for the fulfilled and rejected states.
• **catch(onRejected)**: Attaches a callback for rejection.
• **finally(onFinally)**: Runs a callback once the promise is settled, regardless of the outcome.
Example:

```
myPromise
  .then((value) => {
    console.log("Fulfilled with:", value);
  })
  .catch((error) => {
    console.error("Rejected with:", error);
```

```
    });
```

Promise Chaining

Because then() returns a new promise, you can chain
multiple then() calls for sequential asynchronous
operations. Each then() passes its return value to the next
then() in the chain.
Example:

```
fetchData() // returns a promise
   .then((data) => processData(data))
   .then((processed) => saveData(processed))
   .then((result) => console.log("All
done:", result))
   .catch((err) => console.error("Error:",
err));
```

Key points:
• Return values from then() callbacks become the
fulfilled value for the next then().
• If a promise is rejected at any point, catch() will
handle it.

Error Handling in Promises

Errors thrown inside a then() callback or a reject()
call will cause the promise to become rejected. You can use
.catch() to handle these errors.
Example:

```
doTask()
  .then((result) => {
    if (!result) throw new Error("No
result!");
    return doAnotherTask(result);
  })
  .then((final) => console.log("Final
result:", final))
  .catch((err) => console.error("Caught
error:", err))
  .finally(() => console.log("Operation
finished"));
```

Key points:
- Any error in the chain will skip the remaining `then()` callbacks until it reaches a `catch()`.
- `finally()` is always executed, no matter the outcome.

Promise Methods: `Promise.all`, `Promise.race`, `Promise.allSettled`, `Promise.any`

- **`Promise.all([...promises])`**: Returns a promise that resolves when all of the input promises have resolved, or rejects if any promise rejects.
- **`Promise.race([...promises])`**: Returns a promise that resolves or rejects as soon as one of the input promises settles.
- **`Promise.allSettled([...promises])`**: Returns a promise that resolves after all promises have settled, never rejecting, only providing the outcomes.

- **Promise.any([...promises])**: Returns a promise that fulfills as soon as any promise fulfills, or rejects if all promises reject.

Example:

```
const p1 = Promise.resolve(1);
const p2 = new Promise((resolve) =>
setTimeout(() => resolve(2), 500));
const p3 = Promise.reject("Error!");

Promise.all([p1, p2])
  .then((values) => console.log(values)) //
[1, 2]
  .catch((error) => console.error(error));

Promise.race([p1, p2])
  .then((value) => console.log(value)) // 1
(p1 is faster)
  .catch((error) => console.error(error));

Promise.allSettled([p1, p3])
  .then((results) => console.log(results));
  // [{status: "fulfilled", value: 1},
{status: "rejected", reason: "Error!"}]
```

Multiple Choice Questions (with Answers and Explanations)

1. Which of the following is NOT a state of a Promise? A. pending

B. fulfilled
C. rejected
D. canceled
Answer: D
Explanation: Promises do not have a "canceled" state.
2. How do you create a new Promise? A. `new Promise(callback)`
B. `new Promise((resolve, reject) => {})`
C. `Promise((resolve, reject) => {})`
D. `createPromise(resolve, reject)`
Answer: B
Explanation: The Promise constructor takes an executor function with `resolve` and `reject`.
3. Which method is used to handle successful resolution of a Promise? A. `.catch()`
B. `.then()`
C. `.fail()`
D. `.throw()`
Answer: B
Explanation: `then()` is used for handling fulfilled promises.
4. If a promise is rejected, which method can be used to handle the error? A. `.error()`
B. `.then()` second argument or `.catch()`
C. `.finally()`
D. `.reject()`
Answer: B
Explanation: `catch()` or the second argument of `then()` handles rejections.
5. What does `then()` return? A. `undefined`
B. The same promise
C. A new promise

D. Always a fulfilled promise

Answer: C

Explanation: `then()` returns a new promise, enabling chaining.

6. Which method always executes whether a promise is fulfilled or rejected? A. `.then()`

B. `.catch()`

C. `.finally()`

D. `.done()`

Answer: C

Explanation: `finally()` runs after the promise settles, no matter the outcome.

7. To create a promise that is already fulfilled with a value, you can use: A. `Promise.resolve(value)`

B. `Promise.reject(value)`

C. `new Promise()` without arguments

D. `Promise.done(value)`

Answer: A

Explanation: `Promise.resolve()` creates a promise that is fulfilled with `value`.

8. Which Promise method waits for all promises to fulfill or one to reject? A. `Promise.all()`

B. `Promise.race()`

C. `Promise.any()`

D. `Promise.allSettled()`

Answer: A

Explanation: `Promise.all()` resolves if all promises fulfill; rejects if any reject.

9. If an error is thrown inside a `.then()` callback: A. It is ignored

B. It turns the promise into a rejected state

C. It cancels the promise chain

D. The error is logged automatically

Answer: B

Explanation: Throwing inside `then()` rejects the promise, passing the error to the next catch.

10. `Promise.race()` returns: A. The first promise to settle (fulfilled or rejected)

B. Only if all promises fulfill

C. The last promise to settle

D. A list of all results

Answer: A

Explanation: `Promise.race()` resolves/rejects as soon as one promise settles.

11. `Promise.allSettled()`: A. Rejects if any promise rejects

B. Waits for all promises to settle and returns their results

C. Is the same as `Promise.all()`

D. Returns only fulfilled results

Answer: B

Explanation: `Promise.allSettled()` returns an array of objects describing the outcome of each promise.

12. `Promise.any()`: A. Resolves if any promise resolves, rejects if all reject

B. Rejects if any promise rejects

C. Resolves only if all promises resolve

D. Returns results of all fulfilled promises

Answer: A

Explanation: `Promise.any()` fulfills as soon as one promise fulfills, rejects only if all reject.

13. Which of the following correctly handles an error in a promise chain? A. `myPromise.then(value => { throw new Error("Oops"); }).then(value => ..., err => console.error(err));`

B. `myPromise.then(value => { throw new`

```
Error("Oops"); }).catch(err =>
console.error(err));
```
C. Both A and B

D. Neither A nor B

Answer: C

Explanation: Errors thrown in `then()` can be handled by either a `then()` second argument or a `catch()`.

14.   If `Promise.resolve(42)` is called: A. It creates a pending promise

B. It creates a fulfilled promise with value 42

C. It creates a rejected promise with value 42

D. It throws an error

Answer: B

Explanation: `Promise.resolve(42)` creates a promise instantly fulfilled with `42`.

15.   A promise is considered settled when: A. It's either fulfilled or rejected

B. It's still pending

C. It's canceled

D. After calling `finally()`

Answer: A

Explanation: Settled means the promise is no longer pending — it's either fulfilled or rejected.

16.   If no `catch()` is used and a promise rejects, what happens? A. Nothing, silent failure (in older environments)

B. Potentially an unhandled promise rejection warning

C. The application crashes

D. The promise turns back to pending

Answer: B

Explanation: Modern runtimes warn about unhandled promise rejections.

17.   `then()` callbacks that return another promise: A. Stop the chain

B. Cause the subsequent `then()` to wait for that promise

to settle

C. Cause an error

D. Have no effect

Answer: B

Explanation: Returning a promise in `then()` causes chain to wait until it resolves/rejects.

18.   Which promise method executes only on successful fulfillment? A. `.then()` first callback

B. `.catch()`

C. `.finally()`

D. `.error()`

Answer: A

Explanation: The first `then()` callback runs on fulfillment.

19.   Which statement is correct regarding promises? A. A promise can be fulfilled multiple times

B. A promise state can't be changed once fulfilled/rejected

C. A promise can be canceled out-of-the-box

D. A promise runs code in parallel threads

Answer: B

Explanation: Once settled, a promise's state can't change.

20.   If `doTask()` returns a promise, how to chain another task after completion? A. `doTask().then(result => doAnotherTask(result))`

B. `doTask().addCallback(result => doAnotherTask(result))`

C. `doTask().onComplete(result => doAnotherTask(result))`

D. `doTask().finally(result => doAnotherTask(result))`

Answer: A

Explanation: `then()` is used for chaining tasks.

10 Coding Exercises with Solutions and Explanations

1. Creating and Resolving a Promise

Problem: Create a promise that resolves with the string "Hello World" after 1 second, then log the resolved value.
Solution:

```
const helloPromise = new Promise((resolve)
=> {
  setTimeout(() => {
    resolve("Hello World");
  }, 1000);
});

helloPromise.then((value) =>
console.log(value)); // Logs "Hello World"
after 1s
```

Explanation: We create a new promise that resolves after 1 second. Using then(), we log the fulfilled value.

2. Rejecting a Promise and Handling Error

Problem: Create a promise that rejects with an error "Something went wrong" immediately, and handle the error by logging it.
Solution:

```
const errorPromise = new Promise((resolve,
reject) => {
  reject(new Error("Something went
wrong"));
});
```

```
errorPromise
  .then(() => console.log("This won't
run"))
  .catch((err) =>
console.error(err.message)); // "Something
went wrong"
```

Explanation: The promise rejects instantly. `catch()` handles the error, logging the message.

3. Chaining Promises

Problem: Create a chain of promises:
1. First promise resolves with 2.
2. The next `then()` doubles the number.
3. The last `then()` adds 10.
Log the final result.
Solution:

```
Promise.resolve(2)
  .then((num) => num * 2)     // 4
  .then((num) => num + 10)    // 14
  .then((final) => console.log(final)); //
14
```

Explanation: Each `then()` transforms the value, passing it down the chain.

4. Handling Errors in the Middle of a Chain

Problem: Create a promise chain that:
- First `then()` throws an error.
- Catch the error and log "Caught error".

Solution:

```
Promise.resolve("Start")
  .then(() => {
    throw new Error("Oops!");
  })
  .then(() => console.log("This won't
run"))
  .catch((err) => console.log("Caught
error:", err.message)); // "Caught error:
Oops!"
```

Explanation: The thrown error rejects the promise; `catch()` handles it.

5. Using `Promise.all()`

Problem: Use `Promise.all()` with two promises:
- One resolves to `"A"` after 500ms.
- Another resolves to `"B"` after 300ms.

Log the array of results.

Solution:

```
const pA = new Promise((resolve) =>
setTimeout(() => resolve("A"), 500));
const pB = new Promise((resolve) =>
setTimeout(() => resolve("B"), 300));

Promise.all([pA, pB])
  .then((results) => console.log(results));
// ["A", "B"] after ~500ms
```

Explanation: Promise.all() waits for both promises to fulfill, then logs ["A","B"].

6. Using Promise.race()

Problem: Use Promise.race() with two promises:
- One resolves to "First" after 100ms.
- One resolves to "Second" after 200ms.
Log the winner.
Solution:

```
const fast = new Promise((resolve) =>
setTimeout(() => resolve("First"), 100));
const slow = new Promise((resolve) =>
setTimeout(() => resolve("Second"), 200));

Promise.race([fast, slow])
  .then((winner) => console.log(winner));
// "First"
```

Explanation: Promise.race() returns as soon as fast resolves, logging "First".

7. Using `Promise.allSettled()`

Problem: Create two promises:
- One resolves to `"Success"`.
- One rejects with `"Fail"`.

Use `Promise.allSettled()` and log the array of results.

Solution:

```
const good = Promise.resolve("Success");
const bad = Promise.reject("Fail");

Promise.allSettled([good, bad])
  .then((results) => console.log(results));
/* Logs something like:
[
  {status: "fulfilled", value: "Success"},
  {status: "rejected", reason: "Fail"}
]
*/
```

Explanation: `allSettled()` returns results for both fulfilled and rejected promises.

8. Using `Promise.any()`

Problem: Create three promises:
- Two reject with errors.
- One resolves with `"Found a value"`.

Use `Promise.any()` and log the successful value.

Solution:

```
const p1 = Promise.reject("Nope1");
const p2 = Promise.reject("Nope2");
const p3 = Promise.resolve("Found a
value");

Promise.any([p1, p2, p3])
  .then((value) => console.log(value)) //
"Found a value"
  .catch((err) => console.error(err));
```

Explanation: `Promise.any()` fulfills as soon as one promise fulfills.

9. Returning Another Promise in `then()`

Problem: Write a function `fetchData()` that returns a promise which resolves to `"Data"`. Chain it with `then()` that returns another promise resolving to `"More Data"`, and finally log the result.
Solution:

```
function fetchData() {
  return Promise.resolve("Data");
}

fetchData()
  .then((data) => {
    console.log(data); // "Data"
    return Promise.resolve("More Data");
  })
```

```
  .then((more) => console.log(more)); //
"More Data"
```

Explanation: The second `then()` waits for the returned promise to resolve.

10. Using `finally()`

Problem: Create a promise that resolves after 300ms with "Done", and chain `then()` and `finally()`. Log the resolved value and then log "Cleanup" in `finally()`.
Solution:

```
const delayed = new Promise((resolve) => {
  setTimeout(() => resolve("Done"), 300);
});

delayed
  .then((res) => console.log(res)) //
"Done"
  .finally(() => console.log("Cleanup"));
// "Cleanup"
```

Explanation: `finally()` executes after the promise settles, performing cleanup.

Conclusion

Promises simplify asynchronous JavaScript programming, providing a more elegant solution compared to nested callbacks. By understanding how to create, resolve/reject,

chain, and handle errors with promises, you can write cleaner and more manageable code. Additional methods like `Promise.all`, `Promise.race`, `Promise.allSettled`, and `Promise.any` offer powerful ways to work with multiple promises.
As you master these concepts, you'll be better prepared to tackle more advanced asynchronous patterns, including async/await and advanced concurrency handling.

Async/Await in JavaScript

Introduction

Modern JavaScript provides powerful tools for writing asynchronous code that looks and behaves more like synchronous code. `async/await` is built on top of Promises, allowing you to handle asynchronous operations with cleaner, more readable code.

What are `async` and `await`?

- **`async` keyword**: Declares an asynchronous function. An async function always returns a promise.
- **`await` keyword**: Pauses the async function execution until the promise after `await` settles (fulfills or rejects). It can only be used inside an `async` function.
Key points:
- `async` functions return a promise.
- `await` can only be used inside `async` functions.

- `await` pauses code execution at that line until the awaited promise is resolved or rejected, making asynchronous code appear more like synchronous code.

Example: Converting Promises to Async/Await

Using Promises:

```
fetchData()
   .then(data => processData(data))
   .then(processed =>
console.log(processed))
   .catch(err => console.error(err));
```

Using Async/Await:

```
async function handleData() {
   try {
      const data = await fetchData();
      const processed = await
processData(data);
      console.log(processed);
   } catch (err) {
      console.error(err);
   }
}

handleData();
```

Explanation:
- The `async` function allows using `await` inside it.
- Code reads top-to-bottom, as if synchronous.
- `try/catch` handles errors, replacing `.catch()` from promises.

Error Handling with Async/Await

You can handle errors in `async/await` code by wrapping `await` calls in `try/catch` blocks.
Example:

```
async function getUserData() {
  try {
    const user = await fetchUser();
    const details = await
fetchUserDetails(user.id);
    return details;
  } catch (error) {
    console.error("Error:", error);
  }
}
```

Using Async Functions without Await

Even if you don't use `await` inside an async function, it still returns a promise. The `async` keyword ensures the function's return value is wrapped in a promise.
Example:

```
async function foo() {
  return 42;
}

foo().then(value => console.log(value)); //
logs 42
```

Parallelizing with `Promise.all()` and `await`

If you want to run multiple async tasks in parallel, you can start them first and then `await` their combined results with `Promise.all()`.
Example:

```
async function getAllData() {
  const promiseA = fetchDataA();
  const promiseB = fetchDataB();
  const [dataA, dataB] = await
Promise.all([promiseA, promiseB]);
  console.log(dataA, dataB);
}
```

Converting Callback or Promise Code to Async/Await

Async/await provides a cleaner syntax for asynchronous code, removing "callback hell" and making code more readable.

Multiple Choice Questions

1. What does the `async` keyword do when placed before a function? A. Makes the function run on a separate thread
B. Ensures the function returns a promise
C. Disables exception handling
D. Forces synchronous execution
Answer: B
Explanation: `async` functions always return a promise.

2. Where can the `await` keyword be used? A. Inside any function

B. Only inside functions marked `async`

C. At the global level without conditions

D. In constructors

Answer: B

Explanation: `await` only works inside `async` functions.

3. If an async function does not explicitly return a value, what does it return? A. undefined

B. null

C. A rejected promise

D. A fulfilled promise with value `undefined`

Answer: D

Explanation: Async functions return a promise; if no return value, it resolves with `undefined`.

4. How do you handle errors in `async/await` code? A. Using `.catch()` directly on the async function

B. Using `try/catch` blocks around awaited calls

C. You cannot handle errors in async/await

D. By ignoring them, they disappear

Answer: B

Explanation: Use `try/catch` to handle errors in async/await code.

5. What does `await` do? A. Runs code in parallel

B. Pauses the async function until the promise resolves or rejects

C. Converts a promise into a callback

D. Immediately returns a promise

Answer: B

Explanation: `await` waits for the promise to settle, suspending execution.

6. If an awaited promise rejects and is not caught, what happens? A. The program hangs

B. It throws an error that can be caught by `try/catch`

C. Nothing happens, code continues

D. The process silently fails

Answer: B

Explanation: If you don't handle it, it will throw within the async function, which can be caught by `try/catch`.

7. In async/await, the async function returns: A. A callback

B. A promise

C. A generator

D. A string

Answer: B

Explanation: Always returns a promise.

8. Compare `.then()` chains with `async/await`: A. async/await is just syntactic sugar over promises

B. async/await doesn't use promises internally

C. `.then()` chains can't handle multiple promises

D. async/await is faster than `.then()`

Answer: A

Explanation: async/await is syntactic sugar that makes promise code easier to write and read.

9. Can you use `await` at the top-level of a module (without a function) in standard JavaScript? A. No, not in all environments (as of now), top-level await is new and limited support

B. Yes, always

C. Only in strict mode

D. Only with Babel

Answer: A (As of standard ES2020+ top-level await is allowed in modules, but it's a relatively new feature. The safer historical answer is "No, not in all environments." We'll consider the historical context: top-level await is not widely available in all environments. This question might vary depending on environment. Given standard practice: top-level await is new and only works in modules in modern environments.)

Explanation: Historically, `await` was only allowed inside async functions. Recently, top-level await is supported in ES modules in modern environments, but not universally.

10. What is a common pattern for running multiple async tasks in parallel using async/await? A. `await fetchA(); await fetchB();`

B. `const [a,b] = await Promise.all([fetchA(), fetchB()]);`

C. `const a = fetchA(); const b = fetchB(); await a; await b;`

D. `await Promise.race([fetchA(), fetchB()]);`

Answer: B

Explanation: `Promise.all()` is commonly used with destructuring to run tasks in parallel.

11. If you forget to add `async` before a function that uses `await`, what happens? A. SyntaxError

B. The code runs fine but ignores await

C. It throws a runtime error

D. It returns undefined

Answer: A

Explanation: `await` keyword is only valid inside async functions, otherwise a SyntaxError occurs.

12. Is it possible to mix `.then()` and `await` in the same async function? A. No, they are mutually exclusive

B. Yes, you can mix them, but it's not recommended for readability

C. Only if using polyfills

D. Only in Node.js

Answer: B

Explanation: You can mix `.then()` and `await`, though it may reduce code clarity.

13. How do you handle a rejected promise with async/await? A. Using `try/catch`

B. Using `.error()` method

C. `await` does not handle rejections

D. Using `reject()` in your code

Answer: A

Explanation: Wrap awaited calls in `try/catch` to handle rejections.

14. Which statement is true about async/await and the event loop? A. `await` blocks the entire thread

B. `await` only pauses the async function, not blocking the event loop

C. `await` runs code in parallel threads

D. `async/await` is a synchronous feature

Answer: B

Explanation: `await` suspends the async function's execution but does not block the event loop.

15. If `async function foo() { return "bar"; }`, what does `foo()` return? A. "bar" immediately

B. A promise that resolves to "bar"

C. undefined

D. A rejected promise

Answer: B

Explanation: `async` function returns a promise that resolves with "bar".

16. Can `await` be used to wait for non-promise values?

A. No, `await` only works with promises

B. Yes, it converts non-promises to a resolved promise

C. It throws an error if value is not a promise

D. It blocks forever

Answer: B

Explanation: If a non-promise is awaited, it's treated as a resolved promise with that value.

17. To handle both success and error in async/await: A. Use `await` followed by `.catch()`

B. Use `try/catch`

C. Just `await` without handling errors

D. `finally` only

Answer: B

Explanation: `try/catch` is the typical pattern for handling success and errors.

18. If multiple awaits are sequential and don't depend on each other, how to optimize? A. Run them sequentially always

B. Use `Promise.all()` to run in parallel

C. Use a setInterval loop

D. Use top-level await for all

Answer: B

Explanation: `Promise.all()` runs them in parallel, improving performance.

19. Which keyword is needed to define an asynchronous function? A. `async`

B. `await`

C. `function*`

D. `async function` is a combination, but `async` is the keyword.

Answer: A

Explanation: You prepend `async` to the function keyword: `async function foo(){}`.

20. If `await` is used on a promise that rejects and there's no `try/catch`: A. Nothing happens

B. The async function returns a rejected promise

C. The async function returns a fulfilled promise with

undefined
D. A SyntaxError occurs
Answer: B
Explanation: The async function returns a rejected promise
if you don't handle it.

10 Coding Exercises with Solutions and Explanations

1. Basic Async/Await

Problem:
Write an async function `getMessage` that returns
`"Hello, Async"`. Log the result of `getMessage()`.
Solution:

```
async function getMessage() {
   return "Hello, Async";
}

getMessage().then(console.log); // "Hello,
Async"
```

Explanation:
The async function returns a promise that resolves with the
string. Using `.then()` logs it.

2. Using `await` on a Promise

Problem:
Create a function `fetchNumber()` that returns a promise

resolved with the number 10. Use an async function to
`await` that result and log it.
Solution:

```
function fetchNumber() {
  return Promise.resolve(10);
}

async function printNumber() {
  const num = await fetchNumber();
  console.log(num); // 10
}

printNumber();
```

Explanation:
`await fetchNumber()` waits for the promise to resolve,
then logs the value.

3. Error Handling with Async/Await

Problem:
Create an async function that awaits a rejected promise
and uses try/catch to handle the error, logging `"Error
caught"`.
Solution:

```
async function run() {
  try {
    await Promise.reject("Oops!");
  } catch (error) {
```

```
      console.log("Error caught:", error); //
"Error caught: Oops!"
  }
}

run();
```

Explanation:
The promise rejects, the `await` throws, and the `catch` block handles the error.

4. Sequential Async Calls

Problem:
Create an async function `getData` that:
- Awaits `Promise.resolve("Data1")`
- Then awaits `Promise.resolve("Data2")`
- Logs both results.

Solution:

```
async function getData() {
  const data1 = await
Promise.resolve("Data1");
  const data2 = await
Promise.resolve("Data2");
  console.log(data1, data2); // "Data1
Data2"
}

getData();
```

Explanation:
Sequential awaits handle one after another.

5. Parallel Async Calls with `Promise.all`

Problem:
Fetch two promises in parallel:
- p1 = Promise.resolve("A")
- p2 = Promise.resolve("B")

Use `await` `Promise.all` and log the results.
Solution:

```
async function fetchAll() {
  const [a, b] = await
Promise.all([Promise.resolve("A"),
Promise.resolve("B")]);
  console.log(a, b); // "A B"
}

fetchAll();
```

Explanation:
Using `Promise.all` awaits both results in parallel.

6. Awaiting a Non-Promise

Problem:
Create an async function that awaits a non-promise value (e.g., 42) and logs it.
Solution:

```
async function logValue() {
```

```
  const val = await 42; // 42 is treated as
resolved promise
  console.log(val); // 42
}

logValue();
```

Explanation:
await transforms non-promises into a resolved promise immediately.

7. Returning from Async

Problem:
Create an async function that returns "Done". Log what then() receives.
Solution:

```
async function task() {
  return "Done";
}

task().then(console.log); // "Done"
```

Explanation:
Async function returns a promise; then() logs the resolved value.

8. Using try/catch/finally with Async/Await

Problem:
Create an async function that:

- Awaits a promise that resolves to `"Success"`.
- Logs the result.
- In `finally`, logs `"Cleanup"`.

Solution:

```
async function runTask() {
  try {
    const result = await
Promise.resolve("Success");
    console.log(result); // "Success"
  } catch (e) {
    console.error(e);
  } finally {
    console.log("Cleanup"); // "Cleanup"
  }
}

runTask();
```

Explanation:
`finally` runs after try/catch block, regardless of success or failure.

9. Await in Loops

Problem:
Use a loop inside an async function that awaits a promise each iteration. For simplicity, await `Promise.resolve(i)` and log it.

Solution:

```
async function loopWithAwait() {
  for (let i = 1; i <= 3; i++) {
    const val = await Promise.resolve(i);
    console.log(val); // logs 1, then 2,
then 3
  }
}
```

```
loopWithAwait();
```

Explanation:
Each loop iteration waits for the promise, then logs the result.

10. Converting Promise Chain to Async/Await

Problem:
Given:

```
function fetchData() {
  return Promise.resolve("data");
}
function process(data) {
  return
Promise.resolve(data.toUpperCase());
}
fetchData()
  .then(data => process(data))
  .then(result => console.log(result));
```

Convert to async/await.
Solution:

```
async function handleData() {
  const data = await fetchData();
  const result = await process(data);
  console.log(result); // "DATA"
}

handleData();
```

Explanation:
Async/await replaces `.then()` calls, making code more readable.

Conclusion

Async/await provides a more intuitive, synchronous-like style for writing asynchronous code, simplifying error handling and flow control. By fully understanding async/await, you can write cleaner, more maintainable async JavaScript code. The provided examples, questions, and exercises help solidify these concepts, ensuring you're comfortable applying async/await in your projects.

Conclusion

Congratulations on completing the **JavaScript Handbook: Core Concepts**. By mastering these fundamental concepts, you've built a strong foundation for a successful career in web development. From **data types and operators** to

functions, scope, and closures, each topic you've covered forms a critical piece of the JavaScript puzzle.

As you continue your learning journey, remember that JavaScript is an ever-evolving language. Stay curious, experiment with your own projects, and revisit these concepts as you encounter new challenges. The lessons and exercises in this book will serve as a valuable reference for your future development work.

This book is just one part of a broader series on **JavaScript Mastery**, so stay tuned for more advanced topics like **object-oriented programming, asynchronous programming, and JavaScript design patterns**. Mastery doesn't happen overnight, but with perseverance and practice, you'll achieve your goals.

Happy coding, and keep pushing the limits of what you can create!

About the Author

Laurence Lars Svekis is a renowned web developer, sought-after educator, and best-selling author, celebrated for his extensive contributions to **JavaScript development and modern programming education**. With over **two decades of experience** in web application development, Laurence has become a trusted authority, empowering developers worldwide with his clear, insightful, and hands-on approach to coding concepts.

As a **Google Developer Expert (GDE)**, Laurence is recognized for his work with **Google Apps Script**, where he builds innovative solutions for automation, workflow optimization, and app development. His expertise extends beyond Google technologies, with a deep mastery of **JavaScript, functional programming, asynchronous programming, and modern front-end development**. His unique ability to distill complex concepts into simple, practical lessons has made him a trusted resource for developers at all levels.

Laurence's impact on the developer community is far-reaching. With over **one million students worldwide**, he has become a guiding force for aspiring developers through his **interactive courses, live presentations, and best-selling books**. His teaching philosophy is centered around simplicity, clarity, and hands-on practice, making it easier for learners to understand and apply **core concepts like closures, asynchronous programming, and functional programming**. His content includes **real-world coding exercises, quizzes, and projects** designed to solidify key concepts and promote active learning.

A prolific author, Laurence has published several best-selling books, including guides on **JavaScript fundamentals and advanced concepts**. His books are designed to provide an immersive learning experience, blending theory with practice, while offering clear explanations, coding exercises, and practical use cases. These resources serve as essential guides for both beginner and experienced developers, enabling them to master core JavaScript principles and write clean, maintainable, and scalable code.

Beyond his role as an educator, Laurence actively contributes to the broader **JavaScript and Google Apps Script communities**, where he shares insights, provides mentorship, and fosters collaboration among developers. His hands-on, step-by-step guidance has made him a **trusted voice in JavaScript education**, especially for topics like **closures, async/await, and functional programming**. Passionate about problem-solving through code, Laurence continues to push the boundaries of web development, especially in the context of **modern frameworks like React, Vue.js, and Angular**, where efficient, maintainable, and modular code is essential. His work aims to equip developers with the skills to build effective, scalable applications.

Through his books, courses, and live events, Laurence inspires developers to **unlock their potential, refine their skills, and achieve career success** in the ever-evolving world of software development. His influence extends beyond technical knowledge, offering developers the confidence and clarity needed to approach any coding challenge.

To learn more about his work, access free resources, and explore the world of **JavaScript mastery**, visit BaseScripts.com, where Laurence's passion for teaching, development, and community building continues to shape the next generation of developers.